grace is for sinners

grace is for sinners

written by

serena woods

grace is for sinners
by Serena Woods

www.graceisforsinners.com

Published by Slingshot Creative Media.
slingshot@graceisforsinners.com

All Biblical quotations are from The Message unless
otherwise indicated. The Message: The Bible in Con-
temporary Language by Eugene H. Peterson. Copyright
© 1993, 1994, 1995, 1996, 2000, 2001, 2002. Used by permission of Navpress Publishing Group.

International Standard Book Number: 978-0-615-27875-9
0-615-27875-2
Library of Congress Control Number: 2009902312

Printed in the United States of America

Book cover design and photograph by Ryan Strong.
www.purblinddesign.com.

This book is dedicated to those who have fallen. If you've been there, you know. If you're still there...
hang on.

I wrote this book because of what I learned. I can't explain it away and I can't keep it to myself.

The way you respond to this message is going to depend on where you've been. Most have a hard time putting it down, but some have a hard time with the conviction that they feel. The scriptures kick religion where it hurts. I use a lot of scriptures.

My advice to you is to read the book all the way through and then read it again. It's like watching a movie with a twist at the end and then having to watch it again to pick up on all the clues the author gave throughout the movie.

Most importantly, study the Bible yourself. I'm someone who is opening a window to let in some light, but what you do with what you see is up to you.

You're not going to be the same after this.

Serena

ps: Those of you who start reading this and feel like it was written for you.........It was.

contents

foreword

I don't know if you remember the first time you were hurt by someone, but we all have experienced hurt at the hands of the "others" in our lives. Some of those hurts are easily healed and we go on in life forgetting that they ever happened. But there are other hurts that affect us for a lifetime. Unfortunately there is a lot of hurt being dealt out in the name of Christ and not a whole lot of healing going on.

What's wrong with this picture? I believe it has to do with our perspective of Grace. There isn't a problem with the Grace that God gives us. His Grace is perfect and complete in every way. The Apostle Paul says that God's Grace is big and complete enough for whatever our need happens to be. The issue is with the grace that is passed from one follower to another. For some reason, we in the church have done the very thing that we don't condone in other circles. We've added to the very Message that we've chosen to follow. We've added conditions that God never intended us to follow. The result of these graceless attitudes is a mass driving away from God the very people that God's Spirit is trying to connect with.

Matthew 2:17 quotes Jesus as saying, "Who needs a doctor: the healthy or the sick? I'm here inviting the sin-sick, not the spiritually fit." This has always been the cry of God for those who need life change through a relationship with him. God has always been about drawing people to him through his spirit and through the lifestyles of his followers. The problem we face in America is that there are close to six times as many people outside of the church because of being and alienated by Christ's Followers as there are in church on a regular Sunday morning.

We need a fresh application of God's Grace!

"Grace Is For Sinners" is the documentations of an awesome journey of Grace. The process of God's transformation jumps out at you from the pages you're about to read, and motivates you to take fresh inventory of your own actions and provisions of Grace. I've been able to have the privilege of seeing this process first hand, and I guarantee you the transformation is genuine. Grace is for sinners!

Cal Swenson
Pastor, New Life Church
www.new-lifechurch.org

preface

My friend, Keri, told me a story about a girl who went to her high-school named Erin. Erin was a Christian. People loved and respected her.

When Keri found out Erin was pregnant, she was bombarded with a mixture of emotions. It was confusing to watch someone, who seemed to have it together, fall. It hurt to be let down and it made Keri angry. Especially because Erin *knew* better.

Keri watched as people, both Christians and non-Christians, began to distance themselves from Erin. She struggled with her own emotions and wondered how she should treat her. How does one Christian respond to another who has been caught in life-changing sin?

Keri prayed about it and that night she had a dream. Her dream changed her forever and answered the tough questions about how to handle someone who has fallen.

She dreamt that it was *her*.

This is my story. The names of most of the characters have been changed for their own privacy.

chapter one
a bad beginning

"Even before I was born, you had written in your book everything I would do." - Psalms 139:16

I curled up in a ball on my bathtub floor and let the shower of hot water beat down on my summer skin. I went in there to escape the questions in my daughter's eyes. I didn't want them to see me break down. I wasn't fooling anyone. All three of them were crowded around the other side of the bathroom door calling in to me, asking me if I was okay.

No. Mommy is not okay.

I turned off the water and stepped out onto the bath mat.

I was not alone in my hell. People all over the country were bleeding tears along with me. I was not alone, but I was the one who held the blame. I was a Christian for nine years and never did anything like this before. I didn't think I ever would. I had strong feelings and biting words for people who do what I did and there I sat, being who I hate and still being me, whom I loved. Two separate identities in one small body.

My fall happened quickly. In April of 2005 I was

happy, looking forward to an acting career and experiencing intense spiritual growth. By the second week of May I was sleeping with my friend's husband and three weeks later she knew about it. Three weeks is barely a moment and I did more damage to more innocent people than I ever thought I possibly could.

At night, I like to sit outside and listen to the quiet. I reflect and dream. On that summer evening in August, I went outside and sat staring at my skinny bare legs and painted toes. I let myself be swallowed up by the night. My past was a blur and didn't feel real, my present was a screaming siren of war and my hope was swallowed in the darkness. I wondered, on that night, if hell was just separation from God. I think that most of my conscious awareness was still curled up on the floor of my bathtub and there was little left to deal with the physical reality.

I guess, before I tell you what happened and what I learned, I should tell you where I came from...

༄ 🐛🐛 ༄

I saw myself as an old doll that lost its shine. I've always had an old spirit and I don't remember owning innocence in its purest form. I think it is common for children of abuse to not remember simple childlike innocence.

I am an extremely flawed human being. I have a lot of scars. Many of them were from damage where I was the victim and I have some deep scars where I was not. There is something to be said of wearing the scars of the victim. You always have a team behind you.

I've seen humanity at some painfully low points. My mother was a mentally ill fifteen-year-old runaway when she gave birth to me. She was beautiful and her simple mind made her an easy target for the evil that insecure men were capable of. She was easily controlled at home, but when she went out nobody could control the way other men looked at her. I remember sitting in between her and her boyfriend in the car and the driver of the car next to us smiled over at her. Her boyfriend busted her lip open with his fist and screamed, "Do you want her now?"

When my mom talked to me, her voice was soft and her eyes saw me all the way to the other side. She had a crooked smile that curved up to the left. Her laugh was the kind that bubbled up and spilled on to me and it made me laugh, too. Sometimes we would laugh at laughing. I remember her lap and how there was always a spot for me and I remember the tops of her arms and how I could bury my face in them and smell her. Sometimes she would put me on her hip and hold my hand straight out in front of us and we would dance. She would sing and whoop and bubbles of her laugh would fill the living room. I thought the music was singing for her. I thought she was where the sunshine came from.

It wasn't long before everyone knew that the best way to control my mom was to hurt me. My arm has been the ashtray for a cigarette. I have been dangled over a balcony by my ankle and have sat for what felt like hours with a gun held to my temple. I have heard the heavy breath of a child molester in the dark. There were times where I was beaten and tortured in a drunken rage by my mom's boyfriend. My mother with mascara on her face, a black eye and bloody lip would lie next to my broken body on the floor and plead to me with her eyes, 'Just live through this for me.'

We moved around a lot, sometimes in a trailer park, sometimes in a battered women's shelter. Sometimes we lived in our car.

I was about five or six years old when I was placed in foster care. I spent tortured nights worrying about my mother. There are things she didn't know or understand and she needed me to explain them to her. Years went by and I waited for her to get to a place where she could take care of me. I clung to letters promising that it wouldn't be much longer and that we could be together soon. Three years and eleven foster homes later, we met at the courthouse and I thought that I would finally be able to go home, but instead I found out that she put me up for adoption.

A family in the Midwest adopted me, shortly after. Every aspect of their lives was completely different than anything I ever knew. They had a painfully old fashioned and traditional way of raising children and I found myself plunged, head first, into the private fishin' pond of old fashioned religion. All of my clothes were sorted into piles of 'Acceptable Christian Wear' and 'Unacceptable Non-Christian Wear.' I learned quickly and tearfully what the phrase 'against our religion' meant.

All of the things that made me who I was and linked me to people that I loved and lost on my journey was thrown out like attic garbage and driven out to the farm dump. All connections to the world beyond their eighty acres filled with cows, a couple of horses and some alfalfa were severed. I ended up feeling un-Christian, unclean and angry.

The list of things 'against our religion' was longer than I care to take the time to write, but I'll name a few to give you an idea. I couldn't wear shorts, tanks, earrings, fingernail polish, listen to anything but bluegrass gospel or watch current television. I didn't understand why they thought those things were wrong and the whole thing made me feel like a bad kid when I sized myself up against the list. When I got a few years older and hit the rebellious adolescent stage, I didn't have legs to stand on. People behave according to what they believe about themselves. I was told for years that all the things I loved and felt were good expressions of me were bad. Therefore, I believed I was bad.

There was no use in trying to be good. All hopes for me were shattered before I was even known. There was no standard of an old self to live up to, no belief that I was anything other than what I wasn't supposed to be. If I was getting in trouble for humming a secular pop song I heard at school or getting grilled for jumping around on my front porch because it 'looked an awful lot like dancin' then I give up. And that's what I did. I gave up.

The summer before my senior year in high school I decided to move out on my own. It was a month before I turned eighteen and I was in a place where there was nothing I could do to redeem myself. I moved in with an older friend from work. She lived with her boyfriend whom I immediately discovered was an abusive drunk. I watched him drag her across the floor by her hair and put his hands around her neck to choke the screams out of her. I sat in a corner with my knees pulled to my chin wondering how in the world I got there.

I got a job as a waitress in a diner and enrolled myself in school to finish out my senior year. The quarters I earned didn't go far and my own stamina was hanging by a string that was ready to snap at any moment.

You would think that the snap would come from a comment one of my teachers made on my first day of school. I was in my English class and since that was my favorite subject I planned on him being my favorite teacher. The class introduced themselves by a short interview process lead by the other students. When the teacher found out that I was living on my own he said, 'You won't last long,' and skipped over the rest of my interview.

I wanted to prove him wrong. I wanted one of those movie moments where the student overcomes all obstacles and finishes at the top with big cheers from everybody. However, in those movies, the main character usually has at least one person who believes in them. My teacher missed his opportunity with me.

One night my boyfriend of almost a year broke up with me. He was the last piece of anything good in my life and I was shattered. My friend took me out to the liquor store and bought me a six-dollar bottle of champagne. I drank the entire contents by myself. My ninety-five pound frame was not used to such an overload of intoxication but I was still conscious and didn't want to be. I went to find some weed. That mixed with a bottle of cheap champagne would be the oblivion that I was after. In my hazy inebriation I was the perfect date for a rapist who came in the form of my friend's abusive boyfriend. Fear kept me from telling her and she was the only one close to me at that point, so I held my secret within as it ate away at my self-worth. Something terrible happened to me and I didn't have anyone to tell. This, if you haven't guessed by now, is the point where the string, my lifeline to hope, snapped.

I dropped out of high school and got a crappy studio apartment. I made the local homeless crowd my friends and I got a new boyfriend whom, of course, was a drug dealer. I remember driving down the road and thinking about my life. The thing that bothered me the most was that I had so much of it left.

I decided to go visit one of my old foster mothers. She was one of my favorites. My life is full of things I try to forget, but she is a memory I've always held on to. I liked who I was when I was her daughter and I wanted to go back and reconnect. I gathered up a head full of memories on my three hour drive to her house. When I got there the memories weren't as clear for her. She fostered several other children since me and the stories started running together. This woman was so special to me, but I was just another little foster girl to her.

She did have an interesting memory for me, though. It is something that I've revisited over and over since. She asked me if I remembered telling her about the church van that would stop by my trailer park when I lived with my mom. I did remember. I was about five years old and deep in the darkest part of my life. I would get locked in a scorching bedroom with a box of cereal to feed me through the day, or locked outside to fend for myself all day.

If you can picture me, I was a tiny, malnourished little thing with blue eyes and blonde hair. My clothes hung off of my bony shoulders and my head was full of lice. Every once in a while the church van would come through and about half the time I jumped on and went to Sunday school.

My former foster mother asked me if I remembered what I told her about when we would sing 'Jesus Loves Me'. The hair stood up on the back of my neck because I did remember. The feeling, when I sang that song, was so intense. The only way I, as a little girl, could describe the sensation is 'it felt like I was sitting on Jesus' lap.'

A few months after I visited my old foster mom, I found my biological mother and I got on a Greyhound bus and took off to Georgia to meet her.

She lived in a little shack in a swampy area. It was the sort of house that you drive by and wonder if people actually live there and then you thank God that you don't.

She was married to an old biker and the first time I saw her I didn't quite know how to process what I was seeing. She wore her blonde hair long and frizzy. A black Harley Davidson tank top revealed her tan shoulders and her Levis were tucked into homemade black leather moccasins. She didn't wear any makeup and every finger on both hands wore at least one ring. She's a self-proclaimed gypsy.

I shuffled behind her listening to the soft padding sound that her moccasins made on the tiled depot floor. From the moment she and I got in the car until the moment I left to go home she got me high and fed me Pepsi and 'nerve pills'. I don't remember most of the trip but, to an eighteen year old, having your mom buy your cigarettes for a week was pretty cool.

When I would ask her to tell me some of her memories about our lives together she would say that there were a lot of drugs and a lot of time since then. Then she would convert into a little girl voice and act like she was talking to a little girl. Then she would come back, get nervous and overwhelmed, start to cry and tell me that the memories are too hard.

When I got home I felt more detached and isolated than ever. I always kept a little fantasy about who my mom became and how she was probably a smart business woman and made a decent life for herself. The actuality was that she was the same and her reality existed in places where I never wanted to return.

In August 1995 I found out that I was pregnant. This was the first time I realized I was alive. For the most part, my life left no mark, but being responsible for bringing a new life into the world changed my entire awareness. That realization was promptly joined by panic and a deep sadness.

I imagined all of the pregnant women out there and how they were preparing nurseries and diapers and washing brand new little clothes and folding them away into armoires that smelled like baby powder. Family members were hugging bulging bellies and soon to be daddies were reading stories to belly buttons.

My baby didn't know that she had no future with a mother like me. I felt her grow and kick inside me and my heart sunk because she was full of hope and, to her, there was no telling what kind of wonderful awaited her. I knew the truth and my heart broke with every kick.

What made things worse is that I now had more in common with my mother than I did before. I was an unmarried, homeless high school dropout getting ready to raise a baby on nothing.

I worked as a cashier in a grocery store and one day a woman came through my line and asked me how far along I was. I was so tiny, normally, that most people didn't know that I was pregnant. Her question shocked me out of my robotic and monotonous scanning. She told me that I was so lucky because children are a gift from God.

If that's true, then why in the world would God give me, a worthless teenager, a gift, much less the gift of a child? The possible answers revealed so many implications. My head spun for days going over them.

If all children were gifts, then there are no accidents, only specific purpose. What of my own stupidity and irresponsibility being the cause of the pregnancy? What does that say about the child? Did God want this child here and so used my decisions and failures to bring her here? Or, are there a lot of unintentional people out there who were not part of God's original plan? What do you say to these overwhelming numbers of accidents and how do you know who was supposed to be here and who wasn't? How do you fairly measure the worth and purpose of a life?

Nothing else made sense, so I believed that children were not accidents. They are a gift from God. The biggest implication of all was that God must have seen something in me that nobody else did.

It was strange because I never gave God much of a thought before. I never wanted to live like my adopted parents. It was a stifled and caged-in feeling to me. But, the whole business of God singling me out and giving me this gift that danced in my belly had my attention. This God, whom I never considered, apparently believed in me, and He believed in me right then and there.

That kind of unsolicited and unassuming love was a bit overwhelming. I found a sense of worth and hope. I felt like this big guy had my back and I didn't have to worry about it. That was my moment of coming alive, my moment of salvation. Love saved me. Without question, I was transformed by Love.

chapter two
the beginning of the end

""Simon, Simon, Satan has asked to sift you as wheat..."
- Luke 22:31

The last thing I ever saw myself becoming was a Christian. I couldn't think of one person who claimed to be a Christian that I wanted to be anything like. I would see people change when they either talked about or went to church. I couldn't connect with the way they were behaving. One minute they could be talking about everyday things like traffic jams and sales at the mall, with as much eye rolling and catty chatting as any other group of girlfriends. However, as soon as someone mentioned church or God, they would start talking in Olde English or throw in random ways to be 'rewarded' for their 'tests.' They would punctuate their sentences with creepy smiles and 'amen's.'

When I would come in contact with Christians in their inner circle, it seemed like they weren't connected to reality at all. They were concerned with the way they dressed, the music they listened to and the places they would and would not go. They would strategize, as though they had something to prove, to do whatever they could to be different than everybody else. If I thought about it at all, I would wonder why people had to change so much to believe in a God that was supposed to love them the way they were.

When I did make the decision to believe in Jesus, it was out of a deep need for a rescuer. I figured that changing the way I dressed and the music I listened to wasn't a high price if it meant that I could get some help. I blindly hoped, but I ended up finding something real and it had nothing to do with my appearance and musical preference.

I became aware that the way I looked at things changed. People appeared different to me and my mind opened up to feeling like there were more possibilities to life than I had considered. I had a feeling that there was a lot more 'good' in the world than what I had experienced. The best part, though, was that I was having these free flowing thought conversations with an invisible someone who was intensely intelligent and made me think about things I never thought about before.

I began reading the Bible and journaling my discoveries and questions. I love the idea of keeping a journal. Life is an expedition. A person moves from moment to moment and each one is connected to the one prior and the one after. I like the idea of documenting events so that I can trace back and watch my life unfold.

My third journal entry after I started reading the Bible was dated October 30, 1996. I didn't realize it at the time, but the most important thing that God ever said to me to date was the first thing He used the Bible to say. I was reading one afternoon and I came across a sentence that distinctly stood out, almost like it was its own thing with its own breath. The Bible reads, "Simon, Simon..." but I read, "Serena, Serena..." '[Serena, Serena]. Satan has asked to sift you as wheat, but I have prayed for you,

[Serena], that your faith may not fail. And when you have turned back, strengthen your brothers.' (Luke 22:31-32 NIV).

I made a good friend around that time named Diane. She was one of those who grew up in church and came from generations of the same. She'd say that she went through a rebellious time in her teen years, but I think even a member of Mayberry would have a hard time describing her as rebellious. We didn't have anything in common, except maybe, our sense of humor. She had the best laugh. It was abnormally loud. Everybody loved it and loved to make fun of her for it. I would go over the top trying to be goofy so I could get that laugh out of her.

I respected what she represented. She lived a life that never saw abuse or turmoil. There were a lot of areas in life with which she couldn't identify.

People at church would talk about how God gave them a special verse and they'd share it and talk about it to the group. Their verses pertained to a situation they were going through and were usually encouraging, but mine was quite a bit different. I told Diane about the scripture I got because I wanted to see if it made any sense to her. It didn't and throughout the years in my Bible reading when I would come across that verse it would stick out to me and I'd think, 'There's my verse.'

I began dating Marc right after my daughter was born. I had known him since I was ten and he was always a good friend. He wasn't typically my type, which, at that point, was the biggest attraction for me. He seemed wholesome and what I wanted in someone I'd marry.

Our relationship was on again off again, but we were young and I think there were a lot of times when I would force it to be something more meaningful than it actually was. He seemed like a safe bet to me. He never had a real relationship other than ours and I was amazed when he told me that he only kissed one other girl besides me. He always said that I was and will always be the only one for him. What girl wouldn't swoon at the thought of being loved so deeply that the man who loves her won't touch another woman because he's waiting for her? Something like that happening for me seemed too good to be true. I found out, too late, that he decorated every aspect of our relationship with lies. I'm normally not so easily manipulated, but I desperately wanted what he claimed to offer and I ignored a lot to make it work.

I met a girl named Madeline who immediately became one of the best friends I've ever had. Her background was a lot like mine. We're thirteen days apart, survived horrible childhoods and became Christians in our late teens. Her mother and father divorced when she was little and her mother got remarried to a pedophile. Madeline miraculously found Jesus in spite of her life. Our connection was a deep one and it was based on an understanding of what God can do in an unlikely person's life.

When Madeline began dating Diane's brother, Mitch, he took her to meet his family. They drove to his parent's house and she waited alone in the car while he went in to fill in his family on her past. Her sexual abuse, her teenage drinking and her sexual history were all spelled out while she sat in their driveway. When she was finally summoned she felt naked as she made the long walk from the car to the living room where the strangers, who knew all of her secrets, sat waiting to meet her.

She couldn't help feeling over exposed and insecure. She would try to regain her dignity by acting independent and confident, but it came across as abrasive. Even after their marriage, Madeline never did come to a place where she was on good terms with Mitch's family.

Mitch devoted his time to being the youth pastor at their church while Madeline finished college and spent the rest of her time working alongside him. She loved the kids they worked with and she was proud of her husband's devotion. However, as time wore on it became clear that she was far from what her husband expected of her. Her clothes and hair weren't conservative enough, he didn't approve of her choice of music or movies and he was even worried that being friends with me would be a bad influence on her since I was a 'new Christian'.

At night, after reading to her from the Bible, Mitch would pray for her. He would pray that Jesus would help her want to appear more like a youth pastor's wife, want to grow closer to God and want to be more pure. She felt dirty from her childhood and she felt dirty in her marriage.

She would drive aimlessly for hours to avoid going home. After two years of marriage, she wanted to leave but that would be even worse in everyone's eyes and she didn't want to damage his image and hurt his career. For a solid year, we would meet for lunch almost every day and she would cry, telling me how unhappy she was and how she made a mistake in getting married. She felt like she was a failure and that she was completely trapped.

The day that she discovered that Mitch violated their personal rules of fidelity, Madeline made up her mind to leave him. She would not publicly explain her reasons so as not to hurt his reputation. She would let others think what they wanted about her. Madeline was gone before Mitch got home from work and she gave her explanation in a note that he found taped to the front door.

The aftermath was a witch hunt. She would talk to no one but me. As a result, Mitch called me daily and I would listen to him talk and ask questions for hours. He wanted to know where Madeline was, what she was thinking and if I thought she would come back. I wasn't his friend prior to this. He was a leader at church. Because of his position and popularity, I felt a sense of importance in my newfound role.

He was worried because he said that she knew what the church was like to people who sin and he wanted me to tell her that they could move to a place where nobody knew who they were. He called everybody he could think of from her childhood all the way to her co-workers telling everyone what she did, that leaving him was a sin and that they should all try to contact her and talk some sense in to her.

When the divorce was final Mitch instructed everybody to excommunicate his ex-wife according to 1 Corinthians chapter 5. He told me that I was probably the most important person to her so, as long as she still had me she hadn't lost enough. He told me that if I didn't cut off my friendship with Madeline then I wasn't living according to scripture. I was still a fairly new Christian and I was intimidated by Mitch's intensity.

My relationship with God was important to me, but it was young and I relied on the more mature Christians for guidance. I adopted a lot of their beliefs simply because I didn't know enough on my own. I followed by example. If they told me that gum chewing was a sin, I wouldn't have chewed gum and I wouldn't have a second thought about it. I would do whatever God asked of me and I wouldn't ask questions. If Mitch told me that God wanted me to throw rocks through the window of an abortion clinic, I would have busted out every window in the building and feel honored to have been picked to do it.

When Mitch said that severing my relationship with Madeline was the right thing to do I believed him. I thought the bigger the sacrifice for God, the more meaningful the act would be. I thought that the more it hurt, the more it pleased God. I loved Madeline like a sister, but I loved God more and it never occurred to me that Mitch could be wrong.

When I met with her, she thought we were two girlfriends having a quick coffee break. I watched her lose the last thing that she had. Her entire body wilted and I will never forget watching her eyes as the reality crushed her. When it was over I sobbed as I reported back to Mitch from a pay phone.

Over the years he would tell me how proud he was of me and that he knew it wasn't easy. When I would tell him that I had contact with her he would show surprise and disappointment. Then he would want to know everything I could remember about her and her life. I usually answered all of his questions because her life wasn't how he painted it. I always found that no matter what I said, it would get twisted into something that fit the mold he put her in and I wasn't a strong enough person to argue on her behalf.

He disgraced Madeline in any way he could. He accused her of being a lesbian, he suspected her of having breast implants and he rumored that she was involved in an affair with a man she, later, married. He would, for years, bring her up in conversation, speculate about her behavior and then tie it up with proclaimed hopes that she has somehow submitted herself, though he had serious doubts, to Jesus.

From then on, Madeline's days were filled with familiar faces that would point at her, whisper about her or stare. She didn't trust the intentions or sincerity of anyone. When someone would try to reach out to her, she would hesitate and they would leave. Her hesitation only fueled the gossip fire. Her silence left everything Mitch said about her to be true. Even out of his bed, she couldn't escape his damaging words.

As a man who wanted to remarry some day, he spent eight years trying to get their marriage annulled. He tried to use everything from her being mentally ill to lying about who she was to coerce him to marry her. Neither of which are true. His mission was fueled by his need to be without a blemish. He could not be a divorced man and remarry, that would be adultery and he would lose his ability to preach in his denomination.

Mitch is seen as a victim to those around him, but the reality is that he is a religious bully. He uses smooth words, double talk and warped fragments of scripture to sling like stones. He's a popular guy and he appears blameless because he intimidates with a fast tongue and a contrived smile.

The reality is that he's in a situation that he hates. He doesn't want to be divorced. He wants his life to be and appear as Godly as possible and divorce is a stain that won't come out. Mitch may have his heart in a good place, however, his understanding of grace is so mutilated that it doesn't seem to appear in any area of his life. If he's brutal to others for their lack of spiritual cleanliness, then one can only imagine how hard he is on himself.

About four years after I ended my friendship with Madeline, I was married and living on the East coast. I was reading my Bible and came across a few paragraphs that I knew pertained to that whole situation. I felt sick in my stomach and I knew I needed to contact her. All that time went by, but there wasn't a day when I didn't think about her. I never got past what we did to her. However, I couldn't reconcile Mitch's view with what I felt, so I erred on the side of appearing right rather than being honest. I told myself that doing the right thing was often hard, and I was obligated to 'crucify the flesh' to share the 'hard truth' with someone who it might save.

The verses I read are in Romans chapter 14. "Who are you to judge another's servant? To his own master he stands or falls... Forget about deciding what is right for each other. Here's what you need to be concerned about: that you don't get in the way of someone else, making life more difficult than it already is." I called her and told her I was sorry. I was wrong and she needed to know it. Those were four of the hardest years of her life and this was the first time she ever heard anything like what I was telling her.

In that portion of scripture it says that your judgment can be a stumbling block between them and God and that was exactly what was happening with Madeline. She doubted that God would forgive her because His people didn't show love, mercy or forgiveness. She was turned away. It took her a long time to feel forgiven or to forgive herself because of the people in the church. What a bunch of monsters we can be. I resent being a part of that public character crucifixion.

A few days later I called Mitch's sister and my long time friend, Diane, to tell her about the scripture and the phone conversation. Any mention of Madeline to that family is met with a bristling up that I had grown used to. I called to tell her that we all were wrong this whole time. After I told her about the scripture and Madeline's response, there was a long silence and then she said, "All I can say is that I forgive her and I hope to see her in Heaven some day."

Diane admits that she has a problem with pride, but she rarely sees it at work in her. I responded to her comment saying 'that was pride talking, not forgiveness.' She was silent again and then almost inaudibly she said, 'I get it. I can't talk right now, but I get it.' Then she gave a little laugh saying that I wouldn't believe it, but she gave a message at church the previous Sunday saying that there was unforgiveness in someone's heart and that they would not grow spiritually until it is dealt with. In that moment, on the phone with me, she realized that it was a message for her.

It's interesting how people never think that the message they hear or read is pertaining to them unless it's affirming what they already know or who they already are.

chapter three
road signs

"Keep a cool head. Stay alert. The Devil is poised to pounce..."
- 1 Peter 5:8

Before I was married I remember having this strong feeling that there was such a thing as a soul mate. I knew that mine was out there somewhere and I'd meet him when the timing was right. I imagined I could already feel what our love would feel like. I became painfully aware that I cheated him by giving too much of myself to the wrong people.

I decided that from then on, I wouldn't kiss anyone unless I knew they were the one I would marry. I dated a couple of people during a year and half and didn't kiss either of them because I didn't feel the connection that I knew I would feel and was waiting for.

In March of 1999 Marc sent me tickets to fly out of state and attend a formal ball that the military held annually He promised to buy me a dress with no pressure to be anything but friends. We started talking on the phone a few weeks prior and I wanted to be around him in person to see if he was the one I was waiting for. We were broken up for a year and a half and I thought, since he joined the military and moved out of state, that he could have changed a lot. I agreed to the weekend that promised to charm the part of me that wanted to be adored and cherished.

He lived with another couple that he worked with and one evening they offered me a glass of wine. I didn't drink wine often, but accepted. Marc appeared from the kitchen holding a glass that swirled full of the ruby colored liquid. I didn't find out that he spiked it with vodka until he laughed at me when I fell down the stairs.

He never bought me a dress and he never took me to the ball. Waking up the next morning in his bed was my next clear memory. I was crushed and so ashamed. I felt like my naked body, not my sober choice, was evidence that I made my decision. We were married five days later.

My marriage to Marc was fine. I wasn't euphoric in love, but I wasn't miserable either. I became more confident in myself over the first couple of years and found happiness in being a good mom. I resigned myself to the fact that this is who I chose to marry, no matter the circumstances, and I wanted to make it a good life. He and I were polar opposites, but I saw that as entertaining at best and merely lack luster at worst.

Most of our arguments were about his dishonesty. I learned that I couldn't trust him to tell the truth and I underestimated how much that broke down anything that tied me to him. A lot of resentment hid underneath the surface of my awareness. I didn't have any respect for him and I got pretty ugly when we argued. When I would confront him with his lies I would demand that he admit the truth or admit that he was an idiot.

Our relationship was unhealthy, but the military took him away a lot. Peacefully coexisting was easy. I got to be a mom and he got to be great at his job. I forgot about the notion that there was such a thing as soul mates. I put all of my energy in to my family. The saddest part of our marriage is that neither of us knew the other person. It was a lonely existence.

In 2004 I began traveling a lot. I went to acting classes and auditions between Chicago and Minneapolis. About twice a year I would try to get back to my home state and visit some friends and my family. I was a friend of Anne's for several years. She and Diane were best friends and Diane was the one who set Anne and her husband, Justin, up. He was the drummer for a popular Christian band and toured full time around the country for about eleven years. I knew Justin back then, but he was on one side of a circle of friends and I was on the other.

Anne is known for her generosity and loving heart. She was like a big sister to me. I looked up to her, I annoyed her and I made her laugh. She loved me and she was my favorite part of coming back home. She said that we were kindred spirits and I agreed. I had an open door to her home anytime I wanted. Whenever I came down South, I would use her house as home base for the few days I was in town.

Justin was the type of guy who would try to make Anne's friends feel comfortable. He made sure she didn't have to do much of anything. He was fun and a good buffer because Anne got tired of having company after about two days, and I was usually there for five. What made matters worse is that they had only one daughter and I had three and mine always made the bigger mess. I would clean up after them, but red kool-aid on off-white carpet has a way of making memories. Not to mention, one of my kids always wound up with some sort of bodily fluid on a couch or two.

In February 2005, I returned from an acting competition in Los Angeles where I won 'Actor of the Year'. I was high on possibilities. I met a lot of people in my acting classes. I made some good girlfriends and got hit on by the guys who were several years younger than me. I had such a cocky attitude knowing that they thought I was this hot mom and I ate up the flirty attention.

One day as I was reading my Bible I came across my verse again, this time it was in its original intensity. '[Serena, Serena]. Satan has asked to sift you as wheat, but I have prayed for you, [Serena], that your faith may not fail. And when you turn back, strengthen your brothers.' I e-mailed Diane about it and within a couple of days she sent me a message telling me that she was concerned because Jesus was telling Simon that he was going to deny Him.

It didn't seem possible to me that I would deny Jesus. I had been a Christian for nine years. I studied the Bible two and three times a day. A lot of the mysteries in scripture were becoming clear. I was sharing a lot of them with her through e-mails and, when Mitch would call me, we would end up talking on the phone for hours because he understood the things I was learning and it was exciting. I was on a spiritual high and the idea of denying Jesus was absolutely ludicrous.

In March I got an e-mail from Diane telling me that as she was praying for me she saw a flashing yellow light in her head. She said that she felt like God was yelling at me to 'Stop!' I was confused and annoyed when I read this because that wasn't even close to anything I was hearing from God. God was telling me to not be afraid. He was teaching me that fear keeps you from getting out of the boat. Everything I was getting from God was telling me to keep going.

A couple of days later she wrote me back and apologized because she realized she was wrong. She said that she was praying and God asked her what a flashing yellow light meant. It meant CAUTION. Then He asked her why caution lights are used. They're used to warn people that they are approaching a dangerous intersection. God told Diane to tell me that I'm approaching an intersection where He loses people.

I thought it must be something to do with my acting career. Maybe I'd be tempted with money to cross the line and do something I'm not comfortable with or I'd want to party too hard, so when it came up, I'd recognize it. Months later I would know that entering the intersection wasn't the danger, but finding my way through once I was in the middle was where I was almost lost. I found out that things aren't always as they seem and only my faith would help me navigate my way through.

There was a lot of exciting anticipation welling up inside of me. It was as though my spirit knew something that my head didn't. I knew that I was on the cuff of something big in my life and it was a matter of moments. When I would talk to my husband and friends I would tell them that I thought I was getting ready to be tested like Job, only in reverse. I naively thought that instead of losing everything in my life, I would gain everything I ever wanted.

The memory of my ignorance brings a wry half smile to my lips as I write this. Not because I think it's funny, but because though I got the words right, I was dead wrong on the details.

I did get tested with the test of Job in reverse. I was correct about that, the reversal, however, was that Job was innocent and I was not. If tests are for educational purposes, then Job and I learned the same information. Only, it was personalized to our individual learning styles. We needed to lose what made us feel secure in order for our lives to display the truth of who God is.

I know exactly what Job meant when he said, "Though He slay me, yet I will trust Him." (Job 13:15 NKJV)

On April 11, 2005 I was reading my Bible and for some reason I felt inclined to underline and date a verse that I read. I'll underline things, I've never dated them, but I felt like it was something I needed to pay attention to. It was in 1 Peter 5. 'Live carefree before God; He is most careful with you... You're not the only ones plunged into these hard times. It's the same with Christians all over the world. So keep a firm grip on the faith. The suffering won't last forever. It won't be long before this generous God who has great plans for us in Christ – eternal and glorious plans they are – will have you put together and on your feet for good. He gets the last word; yes He does.'

I wasn't paying attention to the information trend that was developing in my journal. I thought I knew what God was doing, so everything I read or felt was wrapped around my preconceived idea. I heard the words correctly, but I made them mean what I thought they would mean in the context of my awareness.

It never occurred to me that I should be listening to the words of God as though there was something that I didn't know. All of these things that I have shared were designed to assist me after I got lost. I was too busy chasing a rabbit to see the ominous signs, but when I lost the rabbit and lost my way, the signs saved my life.

On Tuesday, April 12, I left for a six-day stay back home. I spent Sunday at my parent's house cleaning some of my old things out of their attic and I found a couple of my old scrapbooks. One was made by one of my foster mothers and the other was an adoption workbook. There were pictures of me and letters from my biological mom. I brought them back to Anne's that evening and sifted through my old memories. I kind of got caught up in it, showing them pictures and reading letters and poems. Anne already heard all of this, so she went on to bed and Justin stayed up to listen to the rest of the story.

It wasn't often that I told my story to people, mainly because it's long and depressing and I don't usually like people to know those things about me. I'm normal and happy so I feel like my story doesn't represent me well. It was getting late and I talked his ear off, so I told him I was shutting up and I went to bed.

On Tuesday morning I got up at 6 a.m. with everything by the door, ready to make the twelve-hour drive home. I was trying to keep the girls quiet because I heard someone sleeping on the couch in the other room. It was too late, though; because I heard them talking and realized it was Justin. I apologized as I ushered them out the front door and he said that he slept downstairs because he wanted to be sure to get to say goodbye. I wondered what Anne thought about that, and then shrugged it off because, though it was out of the ordinary, it was sweet nonetheless. I gave him a side hug and left.

The morning after I got home I received an e-mail from Justin. He thanked me for opening up and said he understood the whole 'hurt kid' thing and he told me about losing his dad when he was eight and about his step-dad who was abusive.

We e-mailed back and forth a few more times talking about our childhoods and then we e-mailed to talk about our days. He legitimately earned my friendship. He was a friend of my girlfriends for years and now I could see why.

Within a week of my return home he sent me a message with a confession that he used to have a 'thing' for me. I thought back to every time I remember him being around and I had no idea he knew I existed.

There was one time in 1998 when I saw him at a function where his band was performing and he caught my eye. I walked up to Anne and told her that I thought Justin was looking good lately. The ice I felt immediately told me that she thought so, too. Anne was six years older than me, about ten inches taller and was a successful business owner. I was a single mom who was trying to go to school and hoping my electricity wouldn't be shut off. That was the end of noticing Justin for me. Not long after that the two were a couple.

I responded to Justin's message telling him that there was a time when I felt the same.

The next few emails were a lot of 'what if' scenarios. I spent some time trying to figure out where in my heart I could place this new friendship with Justin. There wasn't a place for it in my life, so I got the genius idea to create a place making sure it didn't intersect with any other part. I didn't want my marriage to suffer, so I wouldn't tell Marc that Justin and I were talking so much. I didn't think that there was anything to worry about. It just didn't fit in.

Hindsight shows me how dumb I was. I thought I was protecting my marriage from my too-close-for-comfort friendship with Justin. Instead it ended up protecting my friendship with Justin from my marriage.

In a matter of three weeks I went from the idea of me denying Jesus being ludicrous to having an affair. When I think back on that time period, I see a woman, me, behaving extremely out of character and making decisions that were so far from whom I was that it scares me. I can trace thought patterns like a creepy evil seduction that I can't believe I didn't recognize.

There were times when I would think that I should stop e-mailing Justin and then a question would pose itself in my thoughts. Do you have bad intentions? My answer was no, of course not. Then you're okay. Then I'd realize that I wouldn't want anyone to know how close we became. Do you plan on sleeping with the guy? No, no way. Then you're fine. He's a Christian, you're a Christian, you guys can handle this without it going too far. Yeah, yeah that's right. I wouldn't do something like that. I've never done anything like that. I wouldn't let it happen.

But it *did* happen.

In May of 2005 Marc was getting ready to go to school on the East coast. He was receiving a huge promotion that required a four-month long school and I was trying to decide what I wanted to do during that time. I could move to Chicago and audition for four months, hoping that he'd get stationed there so I could stay, I could move to Minneapolis where I was close to my friends from acting school or I could move back home and be around my friends and family. My incongruous friendship with Justin was the deciding factor and I got a summer rental back home.

I still thought that, in spite of our emotional connection, we could be around each other and not be physical. We gave ourselves permission to eventually have a hug. We talked about it like it could contain all of this meaning. The sacrifice that we were willing to make to not be together, even though we both acknowledged that we wanted to, was going to be shoved into that little hug. Neither of us correctly estimated the way our intentions would rip through the fragility of our human nature.

When I lie to myself, I never believe it. Not really. Yet, because I want what I tell myself to be true, I listen and hope. I rely on the promises that I tell myself. I won't let me down. I wouldn't hurt myself like that. One lie that I told myself was that my righteousness would keep me from going too far. I really believed that I was a good person. Maybe I was. Maybe I am. I didn't know this then, but being a 'good person' isn't enough. Having a relationship with Jesus doesn't mean that you won't sin. The lie will always reveal itself. It reveals itself as it defies what it said.

Within thirty-six hours of moving in to my summer rental, my lies revealed the truth about who I was. The steel door between flirting and doing proved to be a flimsy mirage. The ground that I promised myself I wasn't capable of treading was littered with my clothes. Everything I promised myself I wouldn't do happened in between taking them off and putting them back on.

Exactly three weeks later I prayed for the first time since this mess began. I knew that the best policy with Jesus is to be completely honest because He knows the truth anyway. I was in a situation that spun out of my control. My marriage was over and nobody knew exactly why. My friendships were over and they didn't even know the real reason I was pulling out. Even if nobody ever found out about what I did, my life would never be the same. I screwed up, but I did not have to continue. I didn't know what to do, but I did not want to persist. I put my face in my carpet and the only thing I said was, 'Jesus, please help me. I love him.'

I did love him. My head swirled with elation, confusion and sadness. Sometimes we would sit and cry wondering what in the world we were going to do. We shouldn't have known what we knew about each other. But we did. The knowing was done.

The day after my prayer, Justin's close friend and fellow band member found out about our affair. Justin's entire life was built around and determined by the band. It took a split second for the band member to tell Justin that he should know that he could no longer hold the position he was in for eleven years. In that moment, everything that held him together was removed and nothing made sense after that. That evening he went home to tell his wife that he was having an affair. I sat in my living room knowing that the friend I betrayed was getting the worst news of her life. I felt disconnected from reality. I had no real thoughts. I was blank and numb.

Justin agreed to a bizarre sort of 'intervention'. The only people who knew what he did were the two people he hurt the most and a trusted friend and counselor. They took away his phones, computers and any other form of outside contact. He was under twenty-four-hour surveillance and received advice on the phone with their friend and counselor who lived in the D.C. area. They thought it would be best if Justin didn't tell anyone about what was happening. Not even his best friend.

The idea was for him to be able to bounce back with as little image damage as possible. He was babysat during the day until his wife came home from work and then she watched him at night. He couldn't appear to be thinking without being asked what he was thinking about. He couldn't go to the bathroom for too long without someone knocking on the door. He put all of his energy and focus on his two year old daughter.

The original time period was supposed to be two days, but it turned in to a solid month. The only sign of letting up was a daily fifteen-minute walk that he was allowed to take by himself.

During this month I spent most of my time in a mental fog. Every once in a while I would get a quick, hushed phone call from Justin telling me that he was okay, he worried about me and he was hurting with no relief. I usually would let him talk, but sometimes, especially in the beginning, I would try to tell him to not worry about me.

The phone calls would last, usually less than two minutes. It was like getting phone calls from a prisoner.

He risked a lot every time he called. He wanted to give the intervention the time that they deemed necessary because of how strongly he felt about me. He knew he made bad choices and wanted to stick it out and give doing the right thing a chance. He wasn't ready to leave, so, if they knew that he called me, then he would be out whether he wanted to be or not.

When I told him that he didn't have to call, he said that his daughter and these phone calls were the only thing keeping him going. What they were doing to him wasn't accomplishing what they wanted, he became a shell. Nervous and paranoid with no light in his eyes, he wasn't a man anymore.

A few days into Justin's lock down I got a call from Mitch. He asked me if I would write a letter on his behalf because he found a loophole in the annulment system of the denomination he was a part of. Basically, if it could be proved that his ex-wife was a liar and deceived him before and during their marriage then he could get it annulled. They married in 1996 and here it was 2005 and he wanted me to write a letter that damaged Madeline enough to keep a blemish off of his record.

I agreed to write an honest letter that may or may not help him.

In the same phone conversation I told Mitch what I did and what was happening. It was my only connection to someone that would understand the pain I caused. I made the decision to tell the truth and not hold anything back. It must have been scary to him; I don't think he realized that he was talking to a zombie.

I don't remember most of what we talked about. He called almost every night and we would talk for hours. Mostly I felt like I was being beat with a two-by-four. I didn't back away from it, though, because I knew that I did something wrong and if he could do anything to help me, then I would be open to that.

I told Mitch everything. I read him letters. I played him songs. I tried to get him to understand where, exactly, I was so that he would know what to do. His attempts to reach me were like someone trying to talk sense into a drunk, though. I couldn't help him help me. I was dazed and could not connect with reality. No matter what he said to me or what he did, I couldn't undo what I did or un-feel what I felt.

chapter four
lamb lost

"Does He not leave the ninety-nine in the open country and go after the lost sheep until he finds it?" - Luke 15:4

I'm having a hard time trying to find a way to tell my story without damaging the public view of the other characters in my life. I'm not in a place where I need to compare sins and or point fingers. I have enough of my own stuff to worry about. I had an affair with my friend's husband. That fact eliminates the need for examination. There comes a point in the game of tit-for-tat where you're just comparing stench of excrement.

One thing I have learned is that Satan has little power over the believer. He can have his way with a person only under the jurisdiction of God. He can attack, tempt or torment only with a nod from the Almighty. God has given Satan a certain amount of freedom, but if God is with you always, then there is never a time where Satan is acting against you without God's supervision. Even Satan has to answer to God.

A lot of his damage is done with smoke and mirrors. He's a creative liar who plays on your fears and emotions to manipulate you into a place where you are worthless and unable to produce. His ultimate goal is to get you in a place where you cannot affect other believers. He wants to steal your story because he's scared of the power it contains. In the vision that John wrote about in Revelation he says that he saw the believers defeating Satan by the blood of the lamb and by the word of their testimony. If Satan can't undo the crucifixion, then his ultimate focus is going to be on what he can do. He wants to get the believer to a place where they are no longer heard.

It's no question that I am a moral failure. We all are, so I'm not saying anything extraordinary. I fell into a well-spun trap that Satan weaved and it was a horror-flick-tug-of-war to get me out of it. I was a lamb, being ripped apart, limb from limb, at the hands of an entity who knows that the more he can damage me, the worse it will hurt my Father. It is important for you to know that the biggest aid that my horrible demonic attackers received came from the ignorant words and actions of other Christians.

It makes me sick to think of the things that were said to me. It was a absolute message of hopelessness and condemnation that came from the people who were closest to me. So, how do I tell my story and what I've learned without it ending up as a counter-attack against my old friends? My only answer is to make sure that it is said and said again, that this story is not over. We are not the worst thing we have done and until we are dead, our story is incomplete.

When I started to gather my thoughts and notes to answer the overwhelming sense of urgency to write what I've learned in this book, I told God that my old friends will think I've gone off the deep end. God's answer makes me almost laugh every time I tell this part of my story. He said, "Serena, they already do."

In the end of June 2005 Justin called me from a pay phone that was a ten-minute run from his house to tell me that he needed my help. He needed to be able to get far away where he could think and heal. What he did was eating him and the way he was being handled was killing him. He agreed to the intense intervention because of the depth of his failure, but it wasn't working. It was one sided and he couldn't see an end. Four weeks went by and he was sinking into a deep emotional and paranoid pit.

I told him I would see what I could do. I had friends all over the country and I could see if someone would let him stay with them so that he could figure everything out. I found a place in Chicago where my friend was going to be gone for a few weeks. He could crash there as long as he wanted if he helped pay the lease while he used it. The timing worked with my schedule because I was going to be up there for auditions during the first week of July. Justin didn't want anyone to know where he was going to be, so I told no one.

On July 5, 2005, Justin left a letter to Anne explaining his sorrow and guilt lying on the kitchen counter and drove his little girl to pre-school. On the way he told her that he was going away for a little while and that he would be back. She was sitting in her car seat with a sippy-cup of water in her hands watching the summer sky and familiar trees out the window. She stared up at him in the rear-view mirror and said, "I'll find you, Daddy." He stood inside her pre-school for several minutes watching her through the window as she lifted her cup into her teacher's hands. He cried as he watched her, soaking her in.

I drove to Chicago with Justin. We spent three days getting him settled in around my auditions. I felt sorry for this man who was nothing but a shell. He sobbed for his little girl knowing that he wouldn't see her for a few weeks and my heart broke at the damage we did. I didn't know what he was going to do. He had no car, no job, and no one. I've been through some hell in my life and lived through it so I knew he would be fine. But he hadn't and he didn't and when I was leaving he broke down. I've never seen a fear and desperate helplessness like I saw in that man's eyes. He told me that he was afraid of what he would do if he was alone. He didn't feel safe. I needed to get back to pick my children up from my parents. I couldn't stay with him. I couldn't comfort him. I couldn't fix him. I told him he could ride back with me and stay at my apartment until we figured something out. This was our mess. We were in it together.

We never made a plan. We never considered running away together. We never intended to let anyone know of our connection whether we ended it or ignored it. Our affair was too short for there to be any clear thoughts or intentions. We were selfish and detached. The rest of the world, for that short amount of time, did not exist. We felt owned by our connection, powerless to it and we wondered how to get out of it. Then, suddenly, we were in the middle of the destruction we caused.

Part of me wanted to get away from him because I thought he would get a clearer head without me in it. I was a mess, too, and I didn't have anything to give him, except a place to stay safe and breathe and think.

I checked my messages back home and found one from the out of town counselor who was helping Justin and Anne. The counselor wanted to know if I knew of Justin's location. As I listened to the message, the familiar voice filling up my apartment sent Justin shrinking into the dark spare bedroom off the hallway. I followed him in there and found him shutting the shades and pacing in the corner. He pleaded with me to not tell anyone where he was. He wasn't ready to talk to anyone yet. Every noise outside a window or door made him shrink further into himself. I called the counselor back and stood in my living room telling lies to the man I never met while I stared into the windows of Justin's tortured soul.

I went out for groceries and when I came back, Justin told me that he couldn't stay there either. He was paralyzed with fear. I decided to take him to Chicago and the girls and I would stay there for a few days or weeks and it would buy us some time. When we got there, we went through the motions of normal life. Grocery stores, bedtimes, and trips to the city to walk around without fear. Justin started to get some color in his face and I felt a speck of hope. This was a day-by-day existence where two lost people were trying to find their way and not let three little girls know anything different. There was no plan, no real money and we were alone.

After two weeks, Justin was feeling stronger and decided that it was time to call Anne. He stood for two hours on a pay phone in the middle of a mall and paced two foot paces on the square patterned floor. She asked questions. She wanted to know his intentions and she wanted to know where he was sleeping.

When the conversation was over they both knew that he wasn't coming home. On his road of uncertainty, this was the first sense of direction or non-direction that he could count on. It was one path that was not an option.

Anne, up to that point, did everything right. She was willing to keep this man who betrayed her and even saw that his infidelity was partially her fault and thought it could open a door in their marriage that would make them better than ever. She was determined to see the hope in it. She knew the road would be rough and it would take a long time, but she was stubborn and would see it through. I don't know if it was the four weeks of hell Justin went through that broke him, or his love for me that distracted him, or both, but it wasn't enough to make him stay. When he stuck with the intervention for so long, it made her believe that he wanted to work it out. He didn't know what he wanted. He just didn't want to hurt anyone anymore. She told him that on the morning he left she saw relief in his eyes and she knew that this was the day where things would start to change. She didn't know he was leaving. She, now, had been betrayed twice.

Justin didn't know what he was doing. He didn't have a place to stay or a job of any sort and his lack of action forced her to make some major decisions. She did not want their daughter to feel the hurt and rejection that she felt so she got her in to counseling to help with the transition. All Justin wanted in life was to be a good husband, an amazing father and a drummer. That's it. The damage Justin caused was sinking in and he tried to make sense of the destruction. While he pictured his life as a divorcee with split custody of his daughter, Anne was praying to God he would be removed from his little girl's memory.

Toward the end of July, I found out I was pregnant. I don't remember how I felt. I sank further inside myself. August was approaching and school would be starting and I needed to figure out what to do. I didn't have any reason to go home since I would be in a town full of people who knew what I did and the thought of the overwhelming amount of shame I would feel walking around that small town with a swollen belly was too much to wrap my mind around. How much further was my sin going to take me? How lost can a person get? I was learning those answers quickly.

We started searching for a rental in the suburbs. We found a house in a good school district and I knew that I could create a place of peace for my children while

I got through this. It was a great house and Justin began coming to life. He could see himself there. He began looking for a job, which was a task he never thought he'd have to do again. He was a drummer for the same band since he was nineteen and opened a recording studio in his old house. Here he was eleven years later with nothing to offer anyone.

On our first night at the house, we got the girls in bed and went outside to sit in the August night air. As Justin was coming around, I was sinking lower and lower. I sat there feeling swallowed up by the night. I used to be a presence. People loved me. I had something to offer and I destroyed it. I spent the past few weeks in Chicago smudging my pain with vanilla vodka and Dr. Pepper. Now I sat pregnant and I couldn't blur myself any longer. I was forced to think. I was forced to feel. I tried to figure out what I was feeling and it hit me in a wave that swallowed me whole and smothered me. I missed my Jesus. I was that lost sheep that wandered off and I didn't know the way back. I needed Him. I cried for a long time. Justin couldn't reach me and he watched helplessly as I curled up inside myself and shut down.

It was the first day of August, but I gave that year's August a new name. I call it Hell '05.

chapter five
hell '05

"If anyone attacks you, don't for a moment suppose that I sent them..." - Isaiah 54:15

I'm a big reader. I am always reading a book. Usually philosophy or theology or some feel good sort of bubble gum stuff. I'll read my favorite authors and then read their favorite authors and so on. During Hell '05 I went to the bookstore to try to find a book about what I was going through. I needed to know how this sort of thing could happen and what it meant about me. I needed help and books have always been my help.

I learned that you could tell a lot about Christianity by checking out the religious section of the bookstore. There were lots of books about Christians as the victims. I knew for a fact that Christians were not always the victims. I was living proof. I was not a victim, I did something horrible and I needed to find someone who was there and found their way back.

I flipped through pages and pages of books searching for something anywhere near what I experienced and found nothing. I was not a new Christian who was struggling with sin. I was not teetering in my beliefs.

I did not go down some long path of habitual sin. I was a solid, intense and passionate follower of Christ for nine years and I fell, headfirst, off the cliff of righteousness. I never heard of that happening and I wanted answers. I found nothing. I don't know how many Chicago bookstores I stood crying in. I felt angry because I wanted Godly answers to my questions and all I found was a huge hole in the religion section of the bookstore.

I ended up getting a devotion book geared around grace and started trying to have my devotions again. It was a little knick-knack two paragraphs a day token devotional book. I felt like a starving child who was being fed cereal one dry piece at a time. My need overwhelmed the supply and I was sinking.

At this point in my story, I think it's important to say that I was not in a one-day-at-a-time position. The constant tick of the seconds in my life reduced my spirit into powder. Every word from the people I hurt was like a gust of wind and I carried no shield.

One morning I prayed. I told God that I knew what His people said about me, I knew what my sin said about me, but I needed to know what He said about me. I picked up my little devotion book and the scripture it used was from Isaiah 54. I began reading that chapter and about half way through I heard the voice of God. Here is what I read:

> "Your Redeemer God says: I left you, but only for a moment. Now, with enormous compassion, I'm bringing you back.
> In an outburst of anger I turned my back on you — but only for a moment. It's with lasting love that I'm tenderly caring for you. This exile is just like the days of Noah for me: I promised then that the waters of Noah would never again flood the

earth. I'm promising now no more anger, no more dressing you down.

For even if the mountains walk away and the hills fall to pieces, my love won't walk away from you, my covenant commitment of peace won't fall apart. The God who has compassion on you says so.

Afflicted city, storm-battered, unpitied: I'm about to rebuild you with stones of turquoise, lay your foundations with sapphires, construct your towers with rubies, your gates with jewels, and all your walls with precious stones.

All your children will have God for their teacher — what a mentor for your children! You'll be built solid, grounded in righteousness, far from any trouble—nothing to fear! Far from terror—it won't even come close!

If anyone attacks you, don't for a moment suppose that I sent them, and if any should attack, nothing will come of it.

I create the blacksmith who fires up his forge and makes a weapon designed to kill. I also create the destroyer— but no weapon that can hurt you has ever been forged. Any accuser who takes you to court will be dismissed as a liar.

This is what God's servants can expect. I'll see to it that everything works out for the best. God's Decree."

That was the first I heard from God in two months. This time, as I sat there crying, I was crying at the overwhelming presence of mercy. He found me.

This was the first day that I felt any sense of hope at all. I wasn't suddenly healed, far from it, actually. The following day I got an e-mail from my old friend Mitch.

I hadn't talked to him since June when I sent him an e-mail telling him that my computer access was limited, so he would know that I wasn't running or hiding if he wanted to have contact with me. I couldn't count the hours I spent on the phone with him over the years. He was the one who experienced my terrible numbness in the month of June. During that time he said that he wished he could see the spiritual side to what was happening. I didn't know what I expected the letter to say.

The only explanation that I have for what I felt after reading it was that I was under a horrific demonic attack. I'm not talking about negative thoughts or scary pictures. I'm talking about having the sense of being ripped apart by a pack of wild dogs. It was coming from all directions and there was no way I could get free. The fear I felt shrieked through me from some infinite abyss of unfathomable evil and made its way over every inch ripping at me from the inside out. Holding the letter from Mitch in my hands, the shrieks now had powerful words.

Serena,

I have really sought the mind of Christ on this letter. I have sacrificed a quick emotional response for something that is more thought through about which I am more confident. It's also quite frank. I love God's word and it tells me to be frank. It also tells me to speak Truth in love. I pray both are accomplished here.

You mentioned in June, about not knowing who you are. No one knows who you are. I'm thrilled you haven't murdered, but the rest of the 10 Commandments have been broken so readily and so often (still). I see the two of you, fingers raised, flipping God off. I've heard, too, that now the two of you understand Madeline better. You understood Truth before and now you understand deception. Oh, from the heights you've fallen. I just don't get it.

So many people, more and more every day, are weeping over the fact that you are so spiritually deceived. I know that the two of you have weighed this and are fine with it. It's sad, and we hate it, and we hate that the two of you don't (or if you do and are doing it anyways, that's perhaps worse.)

The feelings from various people at various times are anger/sadness/despair/emptiness/ weakness/frustration/fury/etc are over the fact that your innocent children have to witness your sin.

We pray that the sins of their father and mother won't be passed on to them, and we pray that He protects their hearts and minds from you and Justin and from your lives.

Now, we don't abandon, we've been abandoned so I suppose 1 Corinthians 5 is simpler for us that way. I'm not sure how you'll feel when you get this letter. Maybe you're feeling defensive, "but, Mitch, you don't understand this nuance, blah, blah." Or maybe you're just numb, hoping it will all pass. Please know that God's grace isn't cheap. He doesn't cast his pearls before swine.

I pray you seek forgiveness. You can still do the right thing, although I don't expect it as you've become someone else, but it's still a possibility. I'm not sure how this can be redeemed, but I pray God gives you a way of understanding that leads to scraping together what could remain of your life to glorify Him.

Frankly, I hope you don't become famous, as it could hurt our cause so much if people were to know your version of morality. I pray that someday you repent and not try to sneak off somewhere and get involved with a church with ignorant leadership who are excited about you. All the while you're just saying the right words rather than living the right lives.

What hell to have to hide the truth of what you've done. You're guilty prayers of forgiveness are empty. You can't turn from this and at the same time act to all around like nothing is wrong. God sees what is going on inside your heart, and while others may be fooled, He won't be. David and Bethsheba certainly woke up next to each other, but they also wept over the grave of their son and her first husband and lived with guilt forever. David would be slinging stones at the two of you.

Unfortunately, you are now further from the right than you have ever been. I know each of you have started this new life where what you know is trumped by what you feel. I pray God's protection over your children and spouses who never deserved such an evil fate.

I'll close this letter with the same words I gave Madeline in court... I love you and I forgive you.

Mitch

His message came in the name of 'various people, more and more every day' and in the name of 'Christ'. It was a legion of voices in that letter. As the shrieks erupted in every sense of my awareness, I heard a still small voice repeat the words from Isaiah 54: "if anyone should attack you, don't for a moment suppose that I sent them." I wasn't sure I knew the level of faith that can believe God's still small voice over the demonic shrieks of Mitch's words.

I wasn't prepared for what I read. He said he sought the mind of Christ. He took his time writing back to make sure that he said what he believed he was supposed to say. I know these letters. I've written these letters. I've read letters that were sent to others. People pray over letters like these. So why did it open the ground underneath me and let in the unspeakable void? If this had been prayed over and written 'in love,' then why did it escort the absence of hope and show me the inside of my coffin? Dread began a crushing flood into my spirit and filled my lungs with despair.

Mitch told me that nobody knew who I was.

When I think of the people I love, I think of what happens to their faces when they laugh or when they cry. The way the skin around their eyes crinkles into a beautifully familiar pattern of creases. And when they cry, those beautiful creases are the riverbeds for their tears. I think of the freckles on the cheeks that move up an inch when they laugh.

Telling someone that you don't know who they are dehumanizes them. It removes love and familiarity. People do this in order to distance themselves from the emotion of what the other person has caused. It's a form of denial. It's easier to write someone off. When you convince yourself that you don't know who someone is, then you don't have to imagine what he or she must be going through as a result of his or her situation. My identity was removed and I was declared a new creation in the name of my sin.

According to Mitch's letter, my sin drained me of the blood that makes me a mother. The scars across my stomach and the rhythm of my heart were stripped of their life and turned into something that could damage my children. It made me feel like the breath I exhaled contained a poison that would violate the innocence of my babies. The groans of a mother as her children are being ripped from her arms filled my spirit as I looked down at the body that held another innocent life within its ribs.

Mitch is the only person in my history who has used the isolated portion of scripture in 1 Corinthians chapter five to support a corporate turning of backs on a Christian who sins. It was no surprise to find the reference in his letter, but it didn't lessen the burn of the acidic words. What was a surprise was how quickly the decision was made on the part of all of my Christian friends. The decision showed that I was beyond restoration. Beyond help. A price was put on grace and limits were put on me. 'Grace isn't cheap' and I was swine.

He tells me that he prays I seek forgiveness and follows it up by reminding me that I am not me and because I am not me, I must be okay with what I did and not want to be forgiven. What a cruel way to bury me alive. Just tell me that I'm dead and expect me to believe you.

His message to me was that it would be a huge disservice to the life, death and resurrection of Jesus if any one were to hear my story. Yet, another cunning way to steal my hope for future purpose, because even prisoners can hope for a day that they can have their life back. If not, then their only escape is through death. My reason for living was being cut from me with a crude knife made of materials that so many should have recognized as lies.

He made me feel like any attempt I made to find help or to heal would be viewed as a lie as though I was playing a part to get back in. Going to church after this was robbed of the freedom to wilt into the presence of

God, in His house. I was paranoid and scared and had to overcome wondering what people thought of me as I sat on my Father's couch.

Mitch said that David and Bethsheba would be slinging stones at me. Is that because Mitch was slinging stones at me? Are words a form of stones?

I would search the eyes of my Father and wonder if He felt that about me, too. I found His eyes and clung to the small shred of trust that remained as the creases echoed His love for me. Then His eyes looked away as He bent down and dug his finger into the sand.

As I lay in my daughter's twin bed that night and for many nights after, I built a physical barricade using the name of Jesus around my body. If I let any air space between the J and the s, they would get in. I would do that until I fell asleep and again in the middle of the night when they would wake me up.

Something that I know, now, is that Mitch was wrong. He made a critical mistake when he said he was speaking the mind of Christ. When a person claims to be speaking on behalf of Jesus, they carry an unimaginable amount of responsibility. All too often it's some flippant thing people say to sound more religious.

God sees eternity when He looks at us. He knows how the past worked up to this point and where the present will take us. He speaks to us out of his infinite knowledge of eternity and all of its mysteries. That is why God's words are forever, they don't change from one day to the next.

James 3:10 confirms that you can use your words to bless another person or to curse them. Webster's dictionary describes a curse as either a prayer that ushers misfortune or when evil or misfortunes come in response to the words. I can say with every bit of confidence that Mitch's words were intended for evil and did not come from God. Though I cannot say with confidence that Mitch knowingly intended evil, that would speak in to the condition of his heart and I don't know the condition of his heart. I know that he was wrong and that is a symptom of being human.

We can learn something from his mistake. If you are going to speak your mind into the lives of others saying that it's the mind of Christ you better make sure it's a message of love and hope. Otherwise, you could be the sheep whom Satan has disguised himself. Christ words draw you to himself, Satan's words push you back down. That's how you can tell the difference.

Mitch is not a bad person. He's simply a human being who tends to let his own desires and perspective get ahead of his spiritual insight. He may think that he was doing God a favor by writing that letter to me or it's possible that he wrote the letter to earn the affections of Anne, whom he began dating a couple of months later. He's confused, to say the least, and he's made mistakes, but he's still alive and as long as we're alive, we're not finished. To give up on Mitch is to assume that he is the worst thing he's done.

❧ ❦❧❦ ☙

I was several weeks in to my pregnancy and was starting to lose my flat stomach. I didn't feel connected to the pregnancy or anything else around me. I sank into a deep depression. Every once in a while I would resurface and try to figure out what to do. Our lives were in a state of temporary waiting for the next step. We couldn't stay where we were, but this was new territory, we were lost and we didn't know what to do. All of our decisions were made trying to provide security for my daughters.

We weren't a family making a life for ourselves in

that house, we were a separate man and woman who were freaked out at how quickly and thoroughly we destroyed every aspect of our lives. We weren't trying to get away and start a new life together. We were trying to catch up to reality. Though, they weren't the best decisions, we weren't in the best frame of mind. It was survival time and that meant survival by any means possible.

Almost immediately I was forced to admit to myself that the little steps to set up some kind of makeshift resting place weren't going to work. I saw time ticking by and could not see hope or God in my horizon. I carried enough sense about me to know that when rebuilding, if your foundation is corrupt, then whatever you build on top of it will eventually have to come down. We abandoned the lease on the house and moved back to the small town in the Midwest. I crowded in a tiny bedroom with my daughters in my parent's house and he slept on a futon in his mother's living room. I enrolled the girls in school, got a job and began rebuilding.

My husband Marc was in school, cut off from the rest of the world through all of this. I would get to talk to him every once in a while, but only for about ten minutes. Being so cut off from him made me feel like he wasn't an option for help. He refused to leave school and come to me. He suffered in the presence of his classmates and maintained what little control over his life that he could. I'll never understand why he wouldn't leave, but I still think we would have ended up where we are regardless of what he did or didn't do. When he graduated from school he moved directly to his next station. I didn't see him until over a year later and our divorce was already final.

It wasn't long after I moved back that I started receiving threats at work and my children got kicked out of the school they were in as a result of the circulating gossip. It was a small town and, though I didn't know who these people were, they knew who I was and what I did. It was bizarre to go to the store and have people stare at me or physically bump me to let me know that they don't approve of me. They wanted so badly to take a stand for Jesus, but their knowledge of the condition of my heart at that moment was not based on reality. They were taking a stand against a person who goes on to live rather than the sin the person committed that dies in the presence of grace.

I feel for them when I see them now. They don't know what to say or how to behave. They have no closure and no redemption for my sin in their minds. I wish they would come up to me and tell me that I hurt them, or they care about the families that my sin destroyed or that they knew me and cared about me and I let them down. I would understand that because I feel it, too. I cared about our families, too. I let me down, too.

☙ ❧

A lot can be learned from this situation, starting with the fact that anybody can do what I did. Thinking you wouldn't is one of the biggest mistakes you could make. I've been down the wrong road and made it back, I could draw you a map of some of the traps and misconceptions. I could make a list of the equipment that would have made my journey home much easier.

My experience taught me that my 'brothers and sisters' don't want to hear what I have to say. To some, what I've done overrides my potential for spiritual insight or truth. Not everyone says the words, but evading and dividing associations say it for them. It's as if they are terrified of being linked to us. It is eye opening to see an entire group of people walking around with this superstition that a connection with a sinner would somehow taint them. It's likely their driving force is a desire to please their peers and has nothing to do with their actual belief that we could infect them.

I, however, have nothing left to hide. I'm not speaking on behalf of my innocence. I am not innocent and that's the point. There are more people than I know who want me to disappear, but I'm still here and as long as I can communicate, I will. This is my eyewitness account. I have already earned a poor public opinion; therefore by default I don't have anything to lose. I now have a means to discover a legitimate relationship with God that may or may not appear like your orthodox prototype and after my recent experiences I thank God that I'm not like what I've seen. How many of them can say the same? What sort of secrets do they fear people would find out and taint their social positions?

What if we all knew one another's failures? We would be on level ground. There wouldn't be one who could elevate themselves above another as more righteous. Maybe then we could stop condemning, comparing and dividing. This may be wishful thinking because there are still so many ways that we can hurt each other, but I may be on to something, nevertheless. James 5:16 says: 'Make this your common practice: Confess your sins to each other and pray for each other so that you can live together whole and healed.'

Maybe James in the Bible knew that if Mitch and Madeline's friends knew the secret betrayals taking place in their marriage the character death sentence Madeline endured could have been avoided. The result could have left her whole, healed and welcome in the church.

The history remains that Mitch's role in the corruption of their marriage will stay hidden, and Madeline will still be the one who was thrown out. If her fellow Christians, at least, stuck to the self-proclaimed most important piece of behavioral instruction found in the Bible: 'love one another', then they wouldn't have to know all the details. They wouldn't have to be Bible smart, have infallible knowledge of the condition of Mitch and Madeline's hearts or known what was taking place in the spiritual realm, and they still would have ended up right.

You see, if you love someone who will never return it or forgive someone who will never deserve it you still end up blameless. However, if you give up on (the opposite of love; 1 Cor. 13:4) someone who needs you to believe in them or do not restore (the opposite of forgive; Gal. 6:1) someone who could have a significant spiritual impact, then you are guilty of misjudging and condemning and as a result are subject to your own form of justice without wisdom (Matt. 7:2). That is too great a risk and a significant reason why love wins.

chapter six
ode to mrs. moore

*"You gave me life itself, and incredible love. You watched and
guarded every breath I took. But you never told me about this part."*
- Job 10:12-13

In May of 2004 a church in Chicago invited me
to speak at their annual Women's Conference. It was a
weekend conference and I needed to prepare for three
services. It was an overwhelming honor for which I felt
intensely unqualified. Diane was on staff at the church
and thought I would have things to say that would connect with the women who would be there. I made my second appearance on the Today Show and had the sense
if I can be interviewed by Katie Couric in front of millions of viewers on live television, I could speak in front
of their church.

I was on a fairly empty flight headed to Dallas
and used the time to study for the messages I would deliver at the conference. As I sat there with my Bible, a
few books and a scratch pad I overheard a couple of men
talking about their relationships with God in the seats in
front of me. One of the men saw me studying my Bible
and brought me in to the conversation. He told me his
name was Keith and that he was the Executive Director

of an institute that trained people to be youth pastors. A few minutes into the conversation they both agreed that I reminded them of a speaker and author named Beth Moore. I had no idea who she was, but figured I'd look her up later and I went back to studying.

About a week later I was in Chicago for the conference and was spending some time with the pastor and his family. Right away the pastor said that I reminded him of Beth Moore. All weekend long I heard how they thought I was a little Beth Moore. I kind of laughed it off because who knows what that means except, maybe, that she must be terribly fascinating and clever with charming good looks and a witty sense of humor.

A lot happened between May of 2004 and August 2005, as you now know, and I never did find out who Beth Moore was.

⁓᠅᠅᠅᠅⁓

As Justin and I were preparing to move back home to live with our parents, I made one last attempt to find a book that would help me understand my failure and show me the way back. I needed to know how I would get from being the 'swine' that Mitch said I was to being the child of God with a life of purpose that I longed to be. I felt hopeless and I needed hope. I was in the religion section of the bookstore for a few moments when my eyes hit the binding of a book that read, "When Godly People Do Ungodly Things."

I picked it up and skimmed the inside flap until I hit the words, "The final section is directed to those who have been snared by seduction. It points the way back to God, the forgiving Father..." I bought the book and on the way home I noticed the name of the author. That's right. The author's name is Beth Moore.

I began hungrily reading. Within the first chapter I discovered I wasn't alone. There are thousands of people who fell from a place of intense passion for God into absolute sin and failure. The stories are of quick attacks, which leave you reeling and wondering what the heck happened. They aren't stories of long struggles with sinful behavior, but, as Beth wrote, "believers who loved God and walked with Him faithfully for years then found themselves suddenly overtaken by a tidal wave of temptation and unholy assault. Many believers are convinced such things can't happen. '*Not to good Christians.*' They are wrong."

As I continued to read, I could hardly breathe. She began explaining that not all 'departures from Godliness' are evidence of 'defiance, rebellion or proof of inauthenticity.' She explained the torment that someone goes through when they discover that they are capable of falling from the path of righteousness. "Tangling with the roaring lion who is trying his hardest to devour you can constitute real and authentic suffering."

I couldn't believe what I was reading. I felt the hair stand up on the back of my neck when I came to a portion that explained how Christians all over are enduring sudden attacks and finding themselves ensnared by sin. She used 1 Peter 5:9 to support her claim.

My heart began pounding as I put the book down and grabbed my Bible. I flipped feverishly through the pages searching for 1 Peter 5. I found my writing in the margin next to that exact verse. It was the one and only time I dated a scripture that I underlined. The date was the day before I left for my final visit to Justin and Anne's house.

I mentioned in an earlier chapter that maybe God inspired me to date that verse, leaving me clues or landmarks to find my way in the dark. After reading that verse in the context of Beth Moore's book, I know for a fact that God was leaving me clues.

The best clue came next in my reading. It's one of those moments where you discover, without question, a hint of how big God is. He's so big that as your mind starts to approach the idea of His magnitude it malfunctions and zaps into a blank and terrifying awe and you realize, as you squint and move in closer to get a better understanding, you don't even know a fraction of it. I don't know if my flesh and bones could withstand such power. Maybe that's why He stays beyond our understanding. We'd die of awe if He didn't.

Beth talks about the fact that there are rare times when God gives Satan permission to step outside of his usual boundaries and viciously attack one of his children. She talks about Job and the type of attack that was and then she tells the story of Peter. I can't explain what it was like to read my scripture and finally know what it meant for me.

> "Again, we see that Satan had to attain permission to move outside his usual perimeters and launch a full-scale attack on one of God's children: 'Simon, Simon, Satan has asked to sift you as wheat...' To me, the fact that permission was granted is utterly obvious in Christ's use of the word 'when you have turned back, strengthen your brothers.' ... First, we see that Satan can and does seek permission to launch excessive attacks on the children of God. Second, we see that God can and sometimes does grant Satan such permission"

Beth explained that Peter's particular attack was of a specific brand. It was a 'sift'. If a person is called to purpose and contains qualities that would hinder that purpose, then they need to go through a process of change to rid them of those qualities. It's like a new recruit going to boot camp to experience the human breakdown that occurs. The drill sergeants break down the 'man' within the men and rebuild them into soldiers. Beth explains that an encounter with the kingdom of Hell would best accomplish the changing or sifting that needs to take place.

> *"Satan had a sieve. Christ had a purpose. The two collided. Satan got used. Peter got sifted."*

I never heard of anything like this happening. I believed what most of the people I know believe. I always thought that God had a perfect plan for your life and it was your responsibility to know what His will was and to walk in that and if you didn't pray for direction and vision or if you sinned then you were walking away from God. If you walk off on your own by sinning then you were no longer in God's territory, you no longer receive the benefits of God's protection and you are on your own.

I thought that when the Bible said that the way of the believer is a straight and narrow path it meant that it's easy to get off the path and lose your way. I thought that in order to live a righteous, Godly and holy life that it was done by self control. I thought that standing firm in the faith meant refusing to sin. I believed that you could mess up God's plan as easy as telling a lie because lying was outside of His will. If you aren't in God's will or your action in the flesh causes you to slip from the path then His hands are tied concerning your life. The closer you are to God and the stronger that relationship becomes, the less sin you have in your life. Faith equaled strength of will.

It didn't make sense to me that God, who I thought

was nothing but peace and warmth, would allow me to be so viciously and effectively attacked. I especially didn't understand why He would allow it when He knew I'd fall. Beth's book wasn't so much as a blind explanation but, rather, a very timely confirmation. I had all of the information scattered throughout nine years of journaling and whispered into the ears of my friends. To come from someone surrounded in non-controversial sweetness was an effective touch on the part of God who knows me well. Beth wrote that she knows that this sort of thing happens more than we know.

> *"I believe this with all my heart, first of all, because it is congruent with Scripture, and second, because I am convinced it happened to me."*

I have had to completely undo almost everything I thought I knew about God. My moment of truth was when I read 'my verse' in that book and in that context. I had a hard time believing it, even though I was a living, breathing, practically word for word example of the message of Beth Moore's book.

Satan asked to sift me as wheat. God gave him permission. The encounter resulted in me discovering the Truth. It all happened so fast that I was dangling from the noose before I realized I was even on the gallows. There is nothing like that moment when you have nothing left to do but trace your steps backward and see, with gut wrenching clarity, where it started to go south. In that moment I felt like a pawn. Every bit of confidence I had in my knowledge of God was reduced to dust and I felt betrayed.

The pain I was in was so intense and I all I could think of was that He knew this was going to happen and He didn't want my faith to fail. Well, if He knew that this was going to happen then why in the world didn't He tell me what to watch for? He must have known this was the last thing I saw myself doing. I'm not a cheater, I don't betray my friends, I don't hurt people I love. But I did all of those things. And the most piercing question is: If God gave Satan permission to 'sift' me, then that must mean that He didn't do anything to help me.

When God said, 'don't let your faith fail' it wasn't for that moment of sin. It was for the time after. It was for right now as I write these words. Why would my faith fail now? This was all so hard to believe. I lived it and still had a hard time swallowing it.

When other Christians tell me with words or with actions how far gone I am I have to fight against an army of so called 'godly' words and the bullets of demonic accusations gouging my thoughts to believe what I'm hearing from God. When I compare what I thought I knew about God with what I've experienced I have to focus on my faith that God is good. He says 'trust me' as I'm learning that He let Satan attack me knowing full well that I wouldn't stand.

This wasn't a blame game for me. I didn't blame Satan, I didn't blame God, and I certainly didn't blame any of the people involved. This was my doing, my choice, my failure. I've never had a problem with owning that. I've had a problem going from the righteous person I saw myself as to the flawed human being I discovered I am.

I have a recipe for Humble Pie and the main ingredients are your own words and your own actions. It is bitter enough to shrivel your pride and the ingredients are readily available. I had a problem wrapping my mind around the fact that God allowed me to fail in such a way that shifted the foundations so many people counted on.

I don't know if I'll ever completely understand

why, but what I do know, for a fact, is that I discovered a much bigger God through this experience. I can't tell you that these past two years have been easy since I read that book. I've been through hell or purgatory or whatever you want to call it. God had to constantly whisper those words, "Don't let your faith fail" over and over. All the while, my closest Christian friends washed their hands of me entirely as they, through Mitch, told me that they don't believe I ever loved Jesus and that I was spitting on the cross.

One of the most important things that I've learned through this is that everything happens for a reason. God uses everything for His own purposes. God is sovereign and I'll quote Charles Stanley when I say, "As children of a sovereign God you are never a victim of your circumstances."

One afternoon I was sitting on my back porch and decided to s art praising God in the middle of my pain. I tried to think of what I knew was happening as I scanned the sky over the city where all of my old friends live. I remembered that He told me that He was about to rebuild me, so I thanked Him for that and I was trying to think of other things and before I could even form a thought He interrupted my prayer and said, "Serena, I *removed* you."

I felt my heart quicken in my chest and thought about what that meant. No doubt, I was removed, but He said He removed me. Maybe it's because He has a message that He wants me to deliver and my old influences would have too much bearing on it. Maybe He wants me to see the underbelly of religion so that I can call it out and He's using the people closest to me to do it. I may never know God's purposes, but I'll experience them nonetheless.

You may have a hard time approaching the idea that God would allow evil or chaos. You may want to argue that those things would not be in His perfect plan, in fact, that evil and chaos are a departure from God's plan and outside of his circle. If God knows everything beginning to end, if He holds the past in his hand with the present and the future then that means He holds eternity in his hand.

Eternity is like a time trinity: past, present and future in one. The definition for eternity is timelessness or infinite time: time without beginning or end. If God holds in His hand yesterday, today and tomorrow then to Him there is no separation of what was, what is now, and what will be. To Him they all ARE. I'll put it this way, what you were made you what you are and what you are makes you what you will be.

Do you ever wish that you could go back to yourself about ten or twenty years ago and give yourself a pep talk? If I could I would visit myself at age five with burns on my arms, no food in my tummy and a mom whose body is there but her mind isn't. I'd tell myself that one day I will have a great life and that there will be a day when I won't get hurt like that anymore. If I saw myself crying in my bed with no one to comfort me or make me feel safe I would stay by my side until I fell asleep and whisper, "You're not alone, this won't last forever, it won't be long before you're put together and on your feet for good." (1 Peter 5:9-10)

God sees you all together, He sees your 'will be' in your 'right now'. He sees you through eternity. So, when God says He has a plan, He is speaking from a place where His plan is already carried out, so you can't mess it up with your mistakes and you can't make it better with your good works. The 'I AM' has a plan that 'ALREADY IS.' Ecclesiastes 3:14-15 says, "Whatever was is, whatever will be is. That's how it always is with God."

You know when you're reading a good fiction

book and you get invested in the character? Because you, as the reader, have access to her thoughts and her perspective and like no one else in her story you go through her life with her and feel her emotions. You hope with her, cry with her and (if you're a total geek like me) you make yourself some coffee if she's pouring herself a cup of coffee.

About half way through the book, after you've spent days engrossed in and, in some form, living her life, the character goes through some sort of traumatic event. You are so distressed by this and wonder why you subject yourself to this fictional emotion manipulator and you consider not picking the book back up to torture yourself further. However, you do pick it back up and as you read on you find the situation works itself out as situations are known to do you start to see the good things come out of it.

By the end of the story the main character experiences this amazing outcome that wouldn't have been possible without the horrible trauma that happened eight chapters before. You sigh after the closing words, a little sad that it's over, and then decide to read it again.

When you read it the second time and go through her life again, your perspective is different. You know where things are going even though she doesn't. When you reach the moment in her life that is gut wrenching, you can identify because you've been to that place already, but as you watch her writhe and wince under the trauma you are not considering bailing on her like you were before. If you could communicate with her you would be comforting her and telling her that even though she can't see through her circumstances right now you can and you know all of the amazing things that wouldn't be possible without this part of her story.

I see God that way. He's with us on our journey,

but not only has He read our story, He wrote it. There is nothing you can do that He doesn't know is coming. What is an impulse for you in this moment has already happened in His memory.

❧ ✿❧❧✿ ❧

When I was about twelve weeks pregnant we had an ultrasound of our baby. I was watching her move and kick on the television screen and then I saw this face come up out of the blackness. She seemed to be staring right at me as her mouth turned up into a huge smile. Maybe it was an involuntary reaction to a developing nervous system or maybe God used a twelve-week-old fetus to show me His face. I started crying when I realized that this was the first time anyone smiled at me in months.

The stress I was under from the pregnancy, impending divorce and dealing with the continuing demonic attacks caused me to mentally shut down. To this day I have no memory of the better part of that year and a half. Every once in a while Justin will ask me if I remember a movie we rented or the time this or that happened and I have no idea what he's talking about.

I bought a second copy of Beth Moore's book and highlighted all of the things that applied directly to my situation and sent it with a note to Diane. She had nine years of knowledge of my spiritual walk and I was confident that she would be as surprised as I was to learn that this sort of thing could happen.

Other than Marc, She was my one and only outside witness to this story and I was so relieved at the prospect of finally having someone who could attest to the magnitude of what was happening. Neither of us experienced anything like this, so I was anxious to have her on the journey with me.

You would think that scripture could conquer my doubts, but I never heard of anything like this, and the demonic attacks were so intense that I felt like I was drowning. Diane tried for about a month to maintain some e-mail contact with me, but she was consulting with her brother, Mitch, all along the way. I knew that until she was able to trust her own spiritual insight, she would not be any help at all. It makes me wonder if she, too, needed to be 'removed' in order to be who she needed to be.

We e-mailed back and forth several times. One of the first things she asked was: Where are you, spiritually speaking? I gave her a literal answer. I told her that I was being ripped apart by wild dogs and most of the time I wished for death. I explained the terror and dread that I was feeling and that I now understood why people in the Bible got stoned for the thing I did. I told her that I knew that God offered His grace, but that grace is so hard to accept when you can't even forgive yourself.

Maybe she didn't realize that I endured verbal assault from the pit of hell all day long and the things I was hearing in my thoughts were torturing me to the point of not wanting to be in a position to hear them any longer. Her response to me is something I will never forget. She said that what she hears from me is 'self pity and self pity comes from pride and pride is a sin and therefore [I] am not remorseful, [I] sound an awful lot like a victim that is preoccupied with thoughts of death and if [I] consider myself a victim and haven't forgiven myself then [I] cannot possibly be repentant and there is nothing she can do for [me] if [I] haven't come to a place of repentance." Apparently Diane did not read the book I sent. Her brother, Mitch, had a heavy hand in guiding her thoughts and words because he accidently sent me an e-mail he wrote to Diane responding to things I said to her. It's funny how the truth gets exposed sometimes.

I was not in need of someone to tell me that what I did was okay or understandable. I didn't need anyone to tell me that what I did was wrong either. At no point did I think what I did was right. I needed someone to tell me they loved me and they believed in me. I needed to be reminded what is true for the non-Christians you are trying to 'convert' is the same truth for the fellow Christians who find themselves ensnared by sin.

✦

I don't know what causes Christians to shoot their own wounded by taking away the message of the cross. Maybe it's fear or anger or some other natural emotion. Being angry, hurt or confused by a person's sin is not the problem; it's when you use religion for your own emotional agenda. It is anger that causes you to preach the judgment of God, it's the fear of association that causes you to kick the fallen out on his own and it's your own pain that causes you to want the other person to hurt, too.

What we as a body of Christ need to remember is that, until that brother is dead, he is still in the game. Your purpose as his brother in Christ is to offer him your hand and help him back on his feet. It's the sin that you hate and it's the sin that hurt you, not the man. If the man has any kind of knowledge of or relationship with God, I promise you, his failure is tearing him apart and if you don't counter that evil attack with the Godly love inside of you, then his blood is on your hands because you are destroying him. If his faith doesn't fail, however, he will get through it and he will be restored, most likely, to a much better place. But, then if you have crossed him off and separated yourself from him, where does that leave you?

If you believe the message of the cross and are certain of your own salvation, then apply that Truth to your fallen brother. What do you think it means in Philippians 2 when Paul says to work out your salvation? There are probably a few answers to that, but in this context I believe that it means to take that gift of salvation and grace that you preach to the rest of the world and apply it to him. Act it out for him.

A good way to perpetuate the effect of another's sin is in the way you respond to it. If you shut yourself into a mentality or reality that cuts yourself off and requires divided loyalties between believers then you are prolonging the effects of the sin instead of cancelling it out with love. We're told to 'die to sin'. Usually, we take that to mean our 'sinful nature.' We make things mean what we think they mean. Dying to sin also means to not let it linger in your lives once it's made it's way out into the open and identified itself. Don't let it define you when you're the executor or rouse your sinful nature when you're the recipient. Forgive it and get rid of it.

If you were to love out of mercy and hope instead of disown out of hurt and fear then you would be making the sin as if it never happened. That is what forgiveness feels like to the person you are forgiving and it is the best way to pull the plug on Satan's activity. It feels like the sin never happened and your relationship never changed. It's called restoration. Galatians 6:1 says: 'If someone falls into sin, forgivingly restore him, saving your critical comments for yourself.' Instead of expelling him, love him back to where he belongs.

chapter seven
so they'll know

"This is how you'll know that I am God." - Exodus 7:4

Either I went off the deep end, a thought that would no longer surprise me, or God was a lot bigger than I ever knew. Here I have this scripture verse telling me that God gave Satan permission to 'sift' me, the flashing yellow light from Diane's prayers and the clue that I put a date next to that I couldn't explain away. God told me about my failure and nine years later I fail and yet, I was surprised when it happened.

I wanted to give up on myself. If I can do what I did, then was I wrong about God this whole time? My actions confused my friends to the point of making them feel like they never knew me. Did they? Did I know me? Did I even know God? And then that still small voice spoke, 'Don't let your faith fail.' I would think all the way back to that day in October 1996 when He gave me that verse and then fast forward through every minute of my relationship with Him and I am face to face with the fact that He knew all about 'this' back then. I clung to the faith of what I was certain of before the tragedy and began ripping into the Bible and various other books to find some explanations.

The implication was that God allowed Satan to attack one of His followers. I went from three powerful devotions a day, intense prayers and an otherwise spiritual high to being seduced and trapped in sin seemingly overnight. So, my first question was: Does God do this sort of thing?

There are a lot of things, spiritually speaking, that contradict our natural common sense. You might say God's formula is like ours, only in reverse and from the bottom up and usually with a clever twist in the middle.

He tells us that His ways are above our ways and His thoughts above ours, but people still walk around claiming to have infallible certainty that they know the mind of Christ. They make life-altering decisions based on their surefire understanding and leave no room to be completely wrong. I know plenty of people who get something in their head and then put on their blinders only seeing or hearing what confirms their ideas, usually having to stretch scriptures to fit.

If you have positioned yourself to not have your ideas or beliefs challenged on a regular basis, then you are in danger of being a blind fool standing in stagnant water with a bag on your head growing scum on your heart. I'll say, also, that if you have to cut people out of your life who would challenge your decisions and isolate yourself in to a world where you have a tighter grip on who you run in to, then you are in a scary place. How will you learn anything new and grow out of your adversity if you avoid it? Or, even more alarming, do you not think that you have some learning and growing yet to do?

One of the most common ways in which people deal with a catastrophe is to go into denial. Eugene Peterson was talking about this subject in his commentary on

Ezekiel. He writes:

> *"Denial refuses to acknowledge the catastrophe. It shuts its' eyes tight and looks the other way. It manages to act as if everything is going to be just fine. It takes refuge in distractions and lies and fantasies."*

Denial is so dangerous because if you don't acknowledge a festering wound, then you won't seek treatment for it. I've had experiences with people who refuse to admit to there being something unresolved. It's as though they think they'd either be doing God a disservice if they admitted to anger or that something was wrong with their relationship with Jesus if they had lingering human emotions. It's like saying, "I forgive you, but I want nothing to do with you." You're saying what you think you're supposed to say and shutting out the person who hurt you so that you don't have to deal with the emotions and questions. You cancel yourself out. You're pretending to be what you think you should be. You're taking refuge in a lie that says you are no longer affected by the tragedy. The longer you do that, the bigger the fantasy becomes, the less in touch you are with what is real. If you are too distracted by the reality you've created in order to have the 'right' appearance you'll have no reason to believe that you still have some things in you that God needs to work out. If you deny you have a problem, then you will never get rid of the problem.

We have created a religious machine that makes people feel like they have to appear a particular way in order to be thought of as Christians. It makes me feel claustrophobic when I think about the thumb the people in churches are under. You'll say with your mouth one thing and then act out another. Nobody wants to step on toes out of fear of losing church members to the one down the street. Nobody has real answers for the people who hurt or are struggling or who fall into sin. It's a greeting card religion that's long on sentiment and short on meaning.

Life is full of heartbreak and adversity. People will hurt you, things will break down or get lost and you have to go through it. You have to go through this because you learn the hard stuff, the deep stuff, the stuff that matters when you're going through the pain. Oswald Chambers says that you receive yourself from the fires of sorrow. Jesus says that you find your life when you lose it.

Knowing the power of adversity that stirs up change in a person's heart, I have to wonder if God allows such adversity, pain, suffering or sorrow for that purpose exactly. Would God allow something dark or evil if it brought about His purpose?

You can read in the book of Exodus to see an illustration of God causing adversity. God told Moses to bring the Israelites out of Egypt. He filled Moses full of instructions and gave him a few signs to display for Pharaoh in case he resisted. It's clear that God wanted the Israelites to be free. While Moses was there, following God's instructions and displaying the signs, Pharaoh would start to come around and then his heart would harden and he would change his mind. Pharaoh was stubborn and the plagues began.

From the moment that Moses got to Egypt, as God instructed, the Israelites lives got worse. Pharaoh was incredibly unfair and it resulted in the people that God called His own getting beaten. The Israelites blamed Moses and told him to leave and Moses even cried out to God asking why He was treating His people so badly. He questioned God for telling him to rescue the people. At one point he even said, "Does this look like rescue to you?!" (Exodus 5:22) God worsened their condition so that they would have a clear understanding of what they were rescued from.

All of these horrible things happened because of Pharaohs hard, stubborn heart and it says nine times in the book of Exodus that God is the one who made Pharaohs heart hard and stubborn. Why? If it were clearly God's desire for Moses to lead the Israelites out of Egypt, then why would He make Pharaoh's heart hard causing him to be crueler to the Israelites and Moses to unleash plague after plague destroying Egypt? The answer is found several times in Exodus:

> *"You'll know that I am God, your God who brings you out from under the cruel hard labor of Egypt.' (6:6)*
>
> *"This is how you'll know that I am God." (7:4)*
>
> *"And I'll use Pharaoh and his army to put my Glory on display. Then the Egyptians will realize that I am God." (14:4)*
>
> *"I'll use Pharaoh and his entire army, his chariots and horsemen, to put my Glory on display so that the Egyptians will realize that I am God." (14:18)*

So that they will know that He is God, that's why.

You can read Job for another example of God allowing or even, in Job's case, instigating adversity in someone's life.

When Christians see others suffering in their lives, they usually say it's because that person has something amiss. They talk about how God is trying to get their attention or that they have an area of their lives that they haven't turned over to God. Sometimes the fellow Christians will say that the adversity comes because you are doing something right and Satan can't stand it so he attacks you and tries to throw you off. You get angry with Satan giving him a whole lot of credit for what's going wrong in your life and making claims that God's hand isn't in on the plot, but where you go wrong is when you don't recognize that nothing, and I mean nothing, happens outside of God's say so. God gave Satan permission to attack Job. God laid out the rules and Satan had to follow them.

Satan didn't ask about Job, God pointed Job out to Satan asking him if he considered him when he was checking things out on Earth. When Satan told God that He babied Job like a pet, God gave His permission to take everything away from him in order to prove Job's love for God was real. Job lost everything, including his children in some freak accident and all because of a venture between God and Satan.

There's a point later, after Satan did all he could do to attack Job that God pointed him out to Satan again and Satan complained because he wasn't able to lay a hand on Job himself. God gave him permission to do so, short of taking his life. Why would God allow this? If it wasn't about Job, then what is the point of all his suffering? I believe that the answer is much bigger than Job or anything he had on Earth. The answer has to do with what came out of this example. The lessons learned and the illustrations used.

Job claimed that God could do as He pleases because He is God. He said in Chapter ten that he knew of God's goodness and mercy, but nobody ever told him about this part. In one of his rants he even asked, "God and I are not equals; I can't bring a case against Him. We'll never enter a courtroom as peers." (Job 9:32) Basically, we have an entire book claiming who God is. You see an exchange of wrong assumptions made by Job's friends bounced back by his understanding of who God is and the absolute authority He has. God confirms Job's claims about Himself and reinstates Job to a higher place than when he began. God let Job go through all that so that we could know who He was. Job was used because of his devotion to God. His was a devotion that said, and meant, you can do anything with me. Use me.

The third example I'll use is the death and resurrection of Lazarus. This is a classic Sunday school story that I've heard many times. As I understood it, Jesus got word that Lazarus, a good friend of Jesus', was sick. However, He waited a couple more days before He made the long trip to Lazarus' house. When Jesus finally got there, Lazarus was already dead and in his tomb. Jesus is watching Mary and Martha and others mourn the death of his friend and He cries, gets angry and then decides to raise him from the dead.

I thought that Jesus raised him because He was sad and felt bad that He didn't get there sooner, but when I read the story for myself I saw something completely different. John 11:4 says, "When Jesus got the message [about Lazarus being sick], He said, 'This sickness is not fatal. It will become an occasion to show God's glory by glorifying God's Son.'" Later in verses 14 and 15 it says, "Jesus became explicit: 'Lazarus died. And I am glad for your sakes that I wasn't there. You're about to be given new grounds for believing.'" Jesus let Lazarus die and even said that He was glad because this tragedy was an opportunity for everyone who witnessed to see the Glory of God.

This is a side note, but it gives you a picture in to the heart of Jesus. When He got there, Lazarus was dead for four days. When Jesus was around the people He loved mourning the loss of someone He cared about He cried. I believe that through this you can see that Jesus is not disconnected from our emotions. He understands and goes through our experiences with us. When we hurt, He hurts. The human in Jesus relates like only a human can to the bits of 'right now' that seem to overtake us, but the God in Jesus knows what is actually going on and lets us experience what we need to develop new grounds for believing in Him.

The last example I'll use is the cross. That was the darkest hour and was an act of absolute evil and torture to murder the Son of God. Hell rejoiced to find Heaven's Son limp, naked and unrecognizable hanging from a cross. This dark and evil act was allowed by God to bring about His purpose. That purpose was to unite His creation with Himself. We would not want that to happen again, but we thank and worship God for it more than anything else He's ever done.

Here's a challenge for you. Consider all of the players in the story of Jesus' crucifixion from the time He was turned on by Judas to the moment of his death. Consider Judas, the soldiers and the rulers. Think about all the evil that was displayed in these lives. Were they part of God's plan or not? Was it God's will that Judas betray Jesus? Was it God's will for the soldiers to shred his back with the barbaric tools they used? Was it God's plan for Jesus to be murdered? Yes. Yes it was God's plan for these things to happen because it confirms scripture, proving that Jesus is the Son of God.

So, how do you see Judas or the other people who did this? I believe that God used their human condition and Satan's hatred letting them collide into what we now know as the most amazing and beautiful event in the history of Christianity. It is error for you to say that you would have never done it and it's absolutely correct to say, 'But by the grace of God, that could have been me.' When you say, 'but by the grace of God', what you are saying is that if it were not for God's choosing, you would have been the one whose flesh was used.

When you say that you are willing to be used by God, do you have an idea of what you may be used for or do you leave that up to God? What if you play a part that you would never agree to if you were asked? Are there limits to your submission? Do you even have a choice? I know that it's more palatable to imagine God only creating light and peace, but would you think that God could also create the opposite? The answer is yes and Isaiah 45:7 (KJV) confirms it:

> *"I form the light and create darkness, I make peace and create evil; I, the LORD, do all these things."*

God knows us. He knows who will do what in any situation. He also knows who will be with Him in the end and who will not. God uses His omniscient power to bring about His purpose, therefore displaying His sovereign rule over everything. If He knows that, by letting you fall, it will bring about His desired effect, then, He's going to let you fall.

I'm anticipating your reaction to what I'm saying, so I'll let Paul and Job address this:

> *"Is that grounds for complaining that God is unfair? Not so fast, please. God told Moses, 'I'm in charge of mercy. I'm in charge of compassion.' Compassion doesn't originate in our bleeding hearts or moral sweat, but in God's mercy. The same point was made when God said to Pharaoh, 'I picked you as a bit player in this drama of my salvation power.' All we're saying is that God has the first word, initiating the action in which we play our part for good or ill. Are you going to object, 'So how can God blame us for anything since he's in charge of everything? If the big de-*

cisions are already made, what say do we have in it?'
Who in the world do you think you are to second-guess
God? Do you for one moment suppose any of us knows
enough to call God into question? Clay doesn't talk
back to the fingers that mold it, saying, 'Why did you
shape me like this?' Isn't it obvious that a potter has
a perfect right to shape one lump of clay into a vase
for holding flowers and another into a pot for cooking
beans? If God needs one style of pottery especially
designed to show his angry displeasure and another
style carefully crafted to show his glorious goodness,
isn't that all right?" (Paul, Romans 9:14-23, emphasis
mine)

"I'm convinced: You can do anything and everything.
Nothing and no one can upset your plans." (Job 42:1)

If God called me to be a writer with a message He
wanted delivered, but the only way I would understand
the message is by going through the process of failure,
rejection and discovery, then, I believe He would let me
go through that process. When I became a Christian, I
knew God would use my story, my life, and reveal Himself through it. That's what we're taught in churches and
it's what I've always believed. Nobody told me it was possible that God could do more through my failure than
He could through any of my good traits. He didn't show
me who He was through my righteousness, He showed
me who He was through my sin. What I discovered about
who God is and the self-destructive weakness in the
church is the most powerful message and sense of purpose I've experienced.

The only way I could know where the church is
being used by the enemy to make us implode and can-
nibalize each other is by going through the process of

moral failure and having my closest friends be used as an example of how even the best intentioned people can get it all wrong. I gained my life when I lost it, exactly like the scripture says. I don't blame anyone directly. I blame the self-righteous pride lack of spiritual wisdom and a lack in understanding of who God is that make people attempt to destroy their fallen brothers and sisters.

I found myself praying for my old friends several months back. My prayer was a repeat of what Jesus prayed one time. Jesus already knew something that I just learned. It's how you can hate the sin and not the sinner. From the cross, Jesus watched the players play their part in His murder and I watch the players play their part in my story and I'm able to forgive them and myself and move forward to 'strengthen my brothers.' Out of the knowledge of the bigger picture Jesus prayed and I repeated, "Forgive them, Father. They don't know what they're doing." (Luke 23:34)

chapter eight
was it worth it

*"When [the Master] comes, he will bring out in the open and place
in evidence all kinds of things we never even dreamed of—
inner motives and purposes and prayers."*
- 1 Corinthians 4:5

I have always found a bit of comfort thinking that my childhood would enable me to help a wider variety of people. I can identify on a psychological level with people who endured childhood abuse, foster care and adoption. Churches love this kind of story because it's a great before and after picture. I've always been ready to be used as an example of the 'cleaning up' that God can do. So, while I was thinking about what my failure did to my life story I felt like I ruined the whole thing. How could anything I say from here out have any sort of life changing impact? I know now that this sort of thinking is a product of Mitch's letter when he said he prays that nobody ever hears what I have to say because it would hurt the 'Christian' cause so much. That was exactly what Satan would want me to think.

I do have some valid things to say. I know what it's like to be 'that' woman and a person who fought through the flying rocks of condemnation to discover true grace and forgiveness. Not only that, but if my experience can deter one person from the path I chose, I would expose all and lay myself out to be a scrutinized specimen. I can recite the inner dialog that goes on when you're trying to justify your choices. It's so easy to fall into seduction, especially when you think that you are strong enough to get close enough to touch without touching. You can't imagine the 'what ifs' without opening yourself wider and wider to the possibilities. The 'what if's' are no longer un-thought of and in your so called innocent flirting with ideas you've actually been conditioning yourself for the physical act.

I don't think anyone actually understands how much potential they have to do the ungodly. As a matter of fact, I'll say with all confidence that if you think you would never do such a thing as I did then watch out. When you are certain that you would never do something, then there is no reason for you to guard yourself against it. For you, it's a non issue and warrants no attention. That leaves the target wide open and vulnerable for the attack.

In my story, I never considered the future in my choices. I didn't have time. Justin and I went from genuine friendship to flirting to full blown adultery in a matter of exactly three weeks. April 20 to May 11; Wednesday-to-Wednesday. Our physical affair lasted exactly three weeks. May 11 to June 1; Wednesday-to-Wednesday. The only time we considered our future was toward the end of May when we were trying to figure out how we were going to live without each other. We fell in love and that was never considered, but that was our loss, in our mixed up heads, we were still clinging to our righteousness thinking that it was okay to move on from that summer and walk away from each other without anyone knowing what we had done. We thought it would be okay to live a lie since we were the only ones who paid. Or so I thought.

If we spent the rest of our lives living a lie, then what did that mean spiritually? That doesn't work. If we confess what we did, then that would be like joining the two worlds together, the secret place and the reality, therefore solidifying the sin in our minds. Nothing seemed real in that time except our feelings for each other, but they were so out of place that it completely detached us from reality.

After I confessed my sin and my emotional condition to Jesus, He brought it out in to the open within twenty-four hours. I told Him I needed His help and He made the decision for me. No more lies, no more hiding. The two separate realities were made one; I was forced to own my sin, ready or not.

Justin and I were married in October of 2006. From the outside looking in, it would seem that I got what I wanted. We are powerfully and wildly in love. With this in mind, how in the world can I use my life to deter others from this path if I am living what they hope they'll get if they go through with it?

I've thought that my message would have more impact if I were left broken and alone while he worked out his marriage with Anne. I could tell the other girls to run and run fast. If I discovered, after all, that Justin was not the fantasy that I fell in love with, then I could use that to get them to rethink their decisions. I could have been a living-breathing example of things not working out well and the fantasy not being real. A woman in that situation, however, does not believe that she will fail. She'll believe that, although it didn't work out for me, it will for her because what they have is different and no one understands how powerful it really is.

I asked God how I could convey my message without appearing like an absolute hypocrite. How can I tell people to not do this if it, by most accounts, worked out for me? If our time on Earth is but a mist, then I pawned my eternity for a moment of earthly bliss. I felt like anything I could say would be cancelled out by what I had done. That was the end of my story, the source of my peril and the reason for my hopelessness.

Thank God I was wrong. He posed a question: 'Was it worth it?' He clarified: 'Was what happened in your spirit worth all the love and joy with your lover?' My love for God outweighs my love for myself and for another human and I didn't realize that until I had what I wanted in my hands and felt what it felt like to have God turn His face from me. If you are focused on the here and now and living for the moment with no regard for anything beyond your self, then in my case, it was worth it.

If, however, you have even a speck of a relationship with Jesus then, I promise you, no romantic love in its most extravagant brilliance can come close to easing the pain of what it feels like when God turns His face from you. The absolute hopeless devastation of feeling God's cold shoulder is enough to crush the most blatant moral criminal. Even if it's only for a moment, you will never forget the spiritual blackout that rivets your soul with the fire studded jewelry of death in your funeral procession.

Take a leap off a building that is high enough to allow you to come to terms with your own eminent death and watch things get into perspective in record time. Arguments, hurt feelings, lost money and broken promises fade to the equivalent of a generic soda left outside for days to get diluted by rain and candied with the dead bodies of curious flies.

I want to turn people away from this kind of mistake if at all possible. That's why I want to stand at the entrance of this path with a big sign that reads: BEWARE: LOVE ISN'T EVERYTHING AND LOVE ISN'T

ENOUGH.

Romantic love isn't everything because there is so much more to marriage than romantic love. There are things that you will lose that you don't even know are there until you have to savagely cut them out of your body in a divorce. Romantic love isn't enough because no matter the depth of love you have for your lover it will not be enough to shield you from the spiritual pain that you will positively endure, assuming you have any sort of a relationship with God. No earthly love can touch that pain. Romantic love isn't enough to make sin worth the leap and the lack of romantic love isn't enough to make sin worth the risk.

Now, back to God's pressing question: 'Was it worth it?' My answer is as informed as one you will ever receive. I'm not some scorned woman who took a gamble and lost. No. It's not worth it and I know this because *I have what they hope for.*

Make no mistake about my meaning. If you live according to self, then by all means, why give any regard to morality at all? Take moral risks, step on hands and cultivate the 'get mine' mentality. However, this is what I want you to understand: like millions in the bank can ease a multitude of symptoms yet cannot remove cancer from its owners dying body, romantic love can satisfy an immeasurable amount of human desire, but it cannot come close to easing the needs of the spirit.

The truth is that it's not about the people or the happiness or anything else that is attainable with two hands. Obviously, my relationship with my husband wasn't enough to keep me from another man and my friendship with Anne wasn't enough to keep me from her husband. And, as I stood surrounded by the dust and debris of the destruction I caused, I thought of the damage and the pain the people I love endured. The fact was that those things actually weren't what caused me the most sorrow.

I didn't mourn the loss of those relationships like I mourned the loss of my own innocence before God. I got so much out of being his blameless child that, when I was no longer the spotless lamb at His feet, I had a hard time figuring out what exactly I was. In my eyes I went from the charmingly pretty blonde ray of sunshine out making Christianity appear cool to a wrinkled messy hangover with yesterday's mascara smelling of sin and an embarrassment to the cross. I felt like a strung out thief going back to the house I stole from to ask for a second helping. Who did I think I was?

Anyone with an ounce of spiritual discernment can recognize that these thoughts are not from God. I didn't see so clearly then, I needed someone to remind me of what Jesus offers and the only thing I had was a four page letter of condemnation from Mitch and a still small voice that whispered, "Don't let your faith fail." That still small voice was so hard to hear sometimes and as I lay buried in the fight for my spiritual life I would sob because my faith was failing.

All I cared about then and all I care about right now is my relationship with God. I don't care what people think of me or if they like me. Death did that for me. I have an overwhelming urge to share my story and get people, especially the church, to see how damaging they can be to those who sin. I'm writing this because I firmly believe that the people who want to do what is spiritually right in these situations will want to have this knowledge. More than that, I want to be a voice of Truth that can help people who have lost their hope.

For months after my affair, and as I write these words today, Mitch meets with people he thinks may have some kind of contact with me. He makes sure to tell them what happened as he understands it and there was a time when he urged them to follow the example in 1 Corinthians 5 and 'Expel the Immoral Brother.' I heard a definition of gossip recently that said that gossip is used regularly to discredit or demean someone's character in order to validate a personal viewpoint in conflict. Though he may have believed he was doing the right thing, he completely blocked most of the avenues for us to experience the life changing forgiveness and restoration with other Christians. He was 'protecting' the cross like a disabled, disoriented warrior. He effectively set himself up as a roadblock to grace.

There are countless people who have been pushed out by the church because of their sin and a few of them have cited 1 Corinthians 5 as the reason they are no longer welcome. My heart aches at the thought of people not having access to the grace and forgiveness that Jesus died for because of a decision of another brother who said that they went too far. This line of thinking doesn't sit well with me for many reasons and I've spent a great deal of time studying the context around Paul's words to try to gain some balance and insight.

My first step in studying the grounds for excommunicating a brother was to interview anyone who would give me the time. One of the most influential people I was able to interview was Philip Yancey. I asked him if he ever heard of Christians using 1 Corinthians 5 as grounds to publicly dissociate with people who sin. He responded, "Yes, I have. Frankly, I think we need to be very cautious about this. Paul was an apostle, and had a confidence in such pronouncements that very few people should have. Expulsion should be done as a last resort, after grievous sin that even the perpetrator understands as sin, after failed attempts at reconciliation. The church has been notoriously inept at church discipline. We have to start with forgiveness and grace, and go beyond them only when the sinner closes any other avenue."

As I read and reread 1 Corinthians 5 there were four things that stuck out to me and I wanted to get to the bottom of them. The first is that Paul was upset because the church was 'proud' and 'boasting' when talking about a man in their church that was having sex with his stepmother. The second is the process he told them to go through before they kicked him out. The third and fourth are the grounds for this extreme action and its ultimate purpose.

Why would the Corinthians be 'proud' and be 'boasting? The strongest instruction of the New Testament that I've found is the command to love and show love to one another, even when it means to turn the other cheek and offer more than what has been stolen (Mat. 5:39-40). Forgive and forgive quickly. I once heard a definition of forgiveness as taking the consequences of another's sin upon yourself without ever letting them know what it cost you. Galatians 6:1 says, "If someone falls into sin, forgivingly restore him, saving your critical comments for yourself." In the Bible, forgiveness and restoration go hand in hand.

Out of all the spiritual gifts, love is said to be the greatest. In 1 Corinthians 1:10 Paul says, "You must get along with each other. You must be considerate of one another, cultivating a life in common." That would have you to believe that you should go out of your way to keep the peace and stay unified. Later in verse 11 and 13 he writes: "I say this because I hear you're fighting with each other. You're all picking sides... Has the Messiah been chopped up into little pieces?" Paul is clear that they are to not be nitpicking with each other over their differences or drawing divisions in any way.

He later berates that sort of behavior. Chapter three starts out saying, "I am completely frustrated by your unspiritual dealings with each other... Aren't you being totally infantile choosing sides?" Paul is teaching the church how to love one another, he is teaching the message of the cross and the grace and forgiveness it provides and tells the church to not be 'quick to jump to conclusions with [their] judgments' (1 Cor. 4:5).

So, possibly, they are proud to report back to Paul because they are doing as he has taught, they are loving and accepting. They are not bickering or disrupting the peace at all, as a matter of fact, there is a man in their congregation who is living a lifestyle that is quite contrary to what the rest would call 'godly' and they haven't put up a fuss about it at all. They went to the extreme in this one area and they were bragging about their accomplishment.

Paul explains that when someone is living a life of sin, especially a lifestyle of 'scandalous sex' that 'wouldn't even be tolerated outside the church' (1 Cor. 5:1) he should be confronted (5:2). He told them to assemble the congregation and let him be scrutinized by the public (verse 3). If he cannot justify his actions (verse 3), continues his lifestyle of sin and still claims to be a Christian (verse 11) then they are to have nothing to do with him. Let him have a run in with Satan so that his sinful nature can be destroyed and he can be 'on his feet and forgiven' (verse 5).

The 'run in with Satan' is an opportunity for him to feel the displeasure of sin and the disappointment of his peers. When you put a misbehaving child in the corner you want him to feel the discomfort of discipline. You put a child in time out to teach him a lesson, but you never intend to leave him there. Paul never intended for the Corinthians to cast out members of the church for a life term. Paul wants them forgiven and restored.

This doesn't mean that if a person sins, no matter how much it may have hurt you or others, he is to be thrown out. If a person's sin is called out and they confess and ask to be forgiven, then step beyond your personal feelings or selfish agenda to offer them grace and forgiveness. Restore him and move forward showing no recollection of his sin. You're not in charge of who gets forgiven. You are to die to your own selfish nature and offer the grace of Jesus to the fallen. The path of a believer is 'narrow' for a reason. It's hard to deny yourself justice. 1 Corinthians 5 is to be reserved for the extreme cases of a person who makes sin a lifestyle, it is not to be confused with a person whose sin has changed their life.

If you are angry, then say you're angry. If you're confused and can't be around someone because of your emotions, then be honest with yourself and him about those feelings. But don't say you've forgiven someone when you can't carry out the evidence of forgiveness. You are speaking spiritually empty words that only echo between your two broken hearts. Forgiveness for others is a gift that God gives you, it's not something you do, it's something you receive and then give. Imitating that gift is a vile mockery and you would be better off not forgiving.

I know that the ones who have found themselves in most need of this grace are the ones who know how to offer it with a fierce understanding of the gift they are giving. It's a cycle of love that originates with the I AM and is breathed into the body and circulated to all parts. If a part of the body has been pinched off from this life giving, life sustaining circulatory system, then the body as a whole is responsible for the death of the rejected member. The operative word here is 'member.' By divid-ing yourself from a member of your own body, you are making yourself incomplete, effectively causing yourself to be handicapped.

You don't have to like different parts of your body. Without thinking, I can name several parts of my body I wish weren't there, but if I were to cut them off I'd be in worse condition than when I started. So, for the sake of my general wellbeing, I put up with them and find a way to love them because of their overall purpose. I have to make peace with my least favorite parts of my body, be-cause I'm stuck with them, after all.

The more devastating the sin, the bigger the mess. They may still be in the mess they created, but not still be sinning. I'll use my own story as an example to il-lustrate what I'm talking about. I, a married woman, had an affair with a married man. During the three weeks of our sexual immorality I became pregnant. After my re-pentance and public exposure I was in a situation where my husband was across the country in an officer training military school that did not allow him access to anyone outside of the school.

Justin was finalizing his divorce, caring for my children and sleeping on the floor next to the couch where I lay either lifeless or crying night after night. We were not having sex nor were we finding any other form of escape from reality. By the time my husband graduated from his training, he knew what I had done and decided that he no longer wanted to be married to me. However, in the state where I lived, a person could not get a divorce as long as they are pregnant. For months I was trapped in the mess I created. Though I was trapped, I was not living in sin. I was living in the aftermath of sin and that is very different.

Maybe this is why Paul says in 1 Corinthians 4:5-7,

"When [the Master] comes, he will bring out in the open and place in evidence all kinds of things we never even dreamed of—inner motives and purposes and prayers... It's important to see things from God's point of view. I would rather not see you inflating or deflating reputations based on mere hearsay. For who do you know that really knows you, knows your heart?"

The fact is that our view into the hearts of men is limited by our own blind interpretation of what we see and don't see. There are too many ways to be wrong and that's why it's safer to show grace, forgiveness and love.

I'll end this chapter with a quote from Eugene Peterson as he was commenting on the entire first letter to the Corinthians:

> "Paul doesn't disown them as brother and sister Christians, doesn't throw them out because of their bad behavior and doesn't fly into a tirade over their irresponsible ways."

He teaches them how to love one another.

chapter nine
divide and conquer

A constantly squabbling family disintegrates. – Mark 3:22

There are a lot of things that people argue about being right or wrong. There are entire societies that are built around these ideas. Churches sprout and then branch off over the details. Relationships form and fall apart over these beliefs.

You have to be dedicated to finding your own truth, but don't lose sight that it is yours and not necessarily another's. You will find some that agree with you, but because someone is not in agreement does not mean that either of you are wrong. There are absolute certainties in scripture and I'm not suggesting that those can be debated.

Romans 14:2 implies that it is the weak in faith who experience more limitations in their spiritual freedom. It makes sense if you think about a new believer. They have stepped into a completely different sense of awareness and need to find their bearings. Their understanding of who God is and who they are in relation to God may have more of a fear-based association than a freedom based relationship.

If your understanding never moves beyond the here and now into a more open way of thinking you will remain a spiritual runt who is weak in the faith department because your fear keeps you from the water walking experiences that build your faith.

It is a fear that your actions can mess up God's plan or that one false move on your part changes the history books forever. You may be focused on your lack of Godlike abilities and not want to be responsible for altering the universe. So, you may embrace your human limitations, rope them in and nail them down so as to not disrupt God's plan.

You may be thinking all the while that you've got yourself sized up rather accurately when you picture yourself taking out the trash in God's control room and accidentally bumping in to a lever that puts a mountain in the way of God's intentions.

⁓—✿❧❀✿—⁓

When I began on the road to healing after my fall, I thought I ruined everything that God set up for my life. I knew that God had a purpose for me and I believed that my failure messed up that plan. I was taught that you had to line your actions up with God's will so that His plan could be carried out. I tortured myself with thoughts of the damage I caused to God's intent for my life.

You will never hear me say that I deserve to be of value. I don't. The memory of my sin sears my brain with increasing intensity the more I heal. I have letters of condemnation and dismissal, yes, but I also have a letter from Diane begging me to go back to Marc and to go back to God, so that she can dance with me at the welcome home party.

I have memories of the tiny shreds of hope that Mitch and Diane had for me before I closed my eyes to my old life. I can't fairly say that my old friends didn't give me a chance. They absolutely did, but what they didn't know is that all I could see was the web that entangled me. We all wanted to get me out, but nobody could see how.

This healing road has led me down a path of discovery and so many of my misconceptions and fears have been eliminated by studying the scriptures. Romans chapter four talks about God's promise to Abraham.

> *"That famous promise God gave Abraham—that he and his children would possess the earth—was not given because of something Abraham did or would do. It was based on God's decision to put everything together for him, which Abraham then entered when he believed. If those who get what God gives them only get it by doing everything they are told to do and filling out all the right forms properly signed, that eliminates personal trust completely and turns the promise into an ironclad contract! That's not a holy promise; that's a business deal. A contract drawn up by a hard-nosed lawyer and with plenty of fine print only makes sure that you will never be able to collect. But if there is no contract in the first place, simply a promise—and God's promise at that—you can't break it." (13-15)*

I can't mess up God's plan. My failure doesn't ruin me and my achievement doesn't elevate me. This whole thing, life, is not about me or you, it's about Jesus. The story of His love is reflected in the lives of His people, not by what they do, but by what He does with what they do.

Grace twists sin into something that reflects God's love and mercy.

❧

Not too long ago, Justin sent his resume off to apply for a dream job. If he were to be accepted for the position it would require us to move and completely change our lives. There were too many uncertainties to count and once he weighed the potential for disaster it didn't seem worth risking the current 'safe' for the future unknown. However, it was a dream job and the potential was exciting. My husband didn't want to be responsible for sending our family reeling off a cliff just because he got what he asked. However, he felt the possibilities for him to actually be accepted for the position were slim enough he could go ahead and send it.

He daydreamed about it with ten different 'what if' scenarios and tried to not get too excited or invested in the idea. He would bring it up at least twice a day and talk about some little aspect of it, which let me know he was thinking about it more than he wanted to let on. I asked him if he asked God for it and he said no. When I asked him why not, he said he didn't want to ask for something that may not be the right thing for our family, so he asked God to do His will.

I think I've heard every praying person I know either pray like this or talk like this, including myself. What I am seeing here is, while you are aware of your ignorance when it comes to the big picture and your ability to make bad decisions that can alter that picture in a negative way, you are half wrong. You are correct in understanding your ignorance and your ability to make bad decisions, but you are wrong when you think that you can mess up the big picture. Ask yourself a simple question: Who has more power, you or God? It's ludicrous to think that God is sitting on His throne in Heaven watching his creation undoing what He set in to motion.

Tommy Nelson did a study on Ecclesiastes, called 'A Life Well Lived', and talked about this notion that you can mess up God's plan. He said that if that were the case, then he'd never get out of bed. God is not walking around saying, 'Oops, if you hadn't done that, I could have let you have this, or if only you had done this, then you could have stopped that.' This is a fear induced decision-making process that keeps you focused on yourself and the power you have and not focused on your security in God. The borders of common human sense do not bind Him.

If you've ever read 'The Screwtape Letters,' by C.S. Lewis, then you'll have an idea of what I'm talking about here. If you are focusing on yourself then you will not notice that you are elevating yourself to a place of higher power (thinking you can mess up God's plan) because you are too busy congratulating yourself for recognizing your mortal limitations. If you are focusing on your limitations then you are too busy trying to navigate the maze of your limited understanding. Your lack of knowledge creates the walls and fear is your GPS device. Not once have you lifted your eyes to God.

Your limitations or lack of freedom are an expression of your own history and it's a personal journey that you're on. If a person decided they aren't going to drink wine due to their own history with wine, then they don't drink wine for God. If a person does decide to drink wine then they drink it and give thanks to God for great wine.

When you're a believer, you are sitting at the same table eating and drinking (or not drinking) to the same Father. "For instance, a person who has been around for a while might well be convinced that he can eat anything on the table, while another, with a different background, might assume he should only be a vegetarian and eat accordingly. But since both are guests at Christ's table, wouldn't it be terribly rude if they fell to criticizing what the other ate or didn't eat? God, after all, invited them both to the table. Do you have any business crossing people off the guest list or interfering with God's welcome? If there are corrections to be made or manners to be learned, God can handle that without your help." (Romans 14:2-4)

People do cross names off of the invite list, however. They open their mouths in the name of Jesus and make ignorant proclamations as if they are doing God a favor by keeping the 'immoral' person from eating at the same table as those who consider themselves more virtuous. There is not a single person who has the power to undo God's invite or to cancel His welcome. There is not one step in the wrong direction that you can take that would be too far.

The Bible says that the only unforgivable sin is blaspheming the Holy Spirit. Blaspheming is one of those words that has been overused from so many different sources that it is its own entity with a translucent interpretation. To blaspheme is to disclaim. When you blaspheme the Holy Spirit, you are saying He is not real, that you don't believe in him. People can also blaspheme by formally separating themselves from Jesus. It's like a divorce that you put your authorizing signature to.

You can logically deduct that if the only way to get to Heaven is by believing that Jesus is the Son of God, then the opposite, blasphemy, is the only way to not get to Heaven. Jesus explains in Mark 3:28-30 and Matthew 12:31-32 that blasphemy is like sawing off the branch on which you are sitting or severing a connection with the One who forgives. He also explains that if a person rejects the Holy Spirit as a result of a misunderstanding, then it's not the same as blasphemy, which is a conscious decision to divorce the Holy Spirit. If you are 'the bride of Christ' you have to have a full understanding as you denounce your relationship with Jesus.

All of the other stupid and immoral things we do are absolutely forgivable. Even when you're playing dress up and clothe yourself as God and tell a fallen brother that "God's grace isn't cheap' and that 'He doesn't cast his pearls before swine', as ugly and self-righteous as that is, it's still one hundred percent forgivable. It's one hundred percent forgivable because God's grace is free. "And since it is through God's kindness, then it is not by [your] good works. For in that case, God's grace would not be what it really is—free and undeserved." (Romans 11:6) You don't even have to know what grace is to receive it.

✿✿✿✿✿

I have four children and sometimes keeping the peace between them is a full time job. When two of my children come to me with an argument that they can't resolve on their own, I'm never on one side or the other because it's seldom that they are both blameless in the matter. My seven year old could take a toy from my four year old then she retaliates by kicking over the rest of the toys they were playing with. Their peaceful little world is now utter chaos with no identifiable remnants of the fun they were having together before the selfish act.

I'm not concerned about what belonged to whom or who knocked over what or even who was the most innocent in this entire ordeal. It's my job to use their self-indulgent behavior as a tool to teach them how to become good adults. My understanding of their behavior always comes from a place of unconditional and uncontainable love. I can see in to their individual history and understand why they make the choices they make and I can see the potential those current choices have in their futures. I approach them with the bigger picture in mind and I personalize how I relate to them based on their distinctive qualities with the goal of bringing out their best so that they can be the best and have the best.

When we bring our arguments to God, He doesn't go with who came first, who is oldest or who gets in trouble less. We're all His children and He knows who did what and why they did it. He uses our mistakes to teach us spiritual maturity, knowing full well that not one person is completely innocent in the matter. He's not like people. His view is not limited. He doesn't choose sides.

I don't find it easy to not retaliate when someone wrongs me. I'm a scrappy little thing. When I was little I was like a little Robin Hood sticking up for the underdog. When I was about eight years old I went to a major league baseball game with my best friend and her family. There was this family sitting right in front of us with two cute little boys who were somewhere between four and six. As I watched them get settled in their seats and overheard their conversations I quickly despised the father. He was the ultimate of the eighties yuppie's, much like the villains in the Molly Ringwald or John Hughes movies. He was especially mean to his kids. I don't remember what he said, but there was this air about him that I, as an eight year old, felt needed to be knocked down a few notches.

He was wearing a white Izod polo and khaki shorts with penny loafers. I began pinching off small pieces of my pink cotton candy, which I discovered became a more vibrant color when I rolled it into a small ball. I watched him lean slightly forward and I waited until he was sitting back then I tossed the sticky candy ball in between his perfect white shirt and the chair. I could hardly stifle the laugh as I pictured the little pink dot on his white shirt. When he leaned forward again I couldn't see the cotton candy, so I tossed another pinch down the back of his chair as he sat back.

I entertained myself that way until my cotton candy was gone, a pinch for me, a pinch for him. I was only able to get a few small pieces to stick to his back but I figured that it did the trick. Besides, it kept me and my best-friend stifling giggles every time he would lean forward revealing our two or three little spots of retaliation. We were these little bitty bubble gum scented blonde haired girls with big innocent blue eyes and when we giggled you would never suspect us for mischief.

When the game was over and our target of justice stood up to usher his kids through the crowd we watched in horror and delight as his backside rose up out of the chair. Right before our eyes we found every single ball of candy we tossed not stuck to his shirt, as I intended, but to every inch of his khaki shorts. His rear end was dramatically confettied with our candy bullets. We erupted in a mixture of shocked laughter and jaw dropping horror at the magnitude of our efforts as he walked his little boys out of the aisle of seats and down the stairs. Our eyes were glued to his backside until he maneuvered his way through the crowd and out of sight.

I was around the same age, about third grade, and rode the school bus with the same best friend and there was a sixth grader who treated everyone like they were her underlings. She was bossy and mean and I took it upon myself to knock her down a few pegs. Again, it was the eighties and back then big hair was possibly the most important fashion statement you could make. Her hair was always back combed and hair sprayed to colossal brunette perfection. The fashion statement for us third graders was our cherry flavored Vaseline squeeze tubes. I decided to let our fashion statements collide and by the time the bus pulled in to school, most of the contents of my lip gloss was ribboned through her hair with tiny shards of white notebook paper clinging to the cherry scented goo.

Being an ugly person has its own punishment and if that internal justice isn't enough then there's nothing I can do that could touch them. Besides, sometimes the hardest people to love are those who need it the most.

As believers, we are supposed to be a family. We're the children and God is the Father. We are so completely different from one another and more often than not the only thing that binds us together is our Father. The Bible warns against fighting amongst ourselves, drawing divisions and setting up camps of opposition. Paul wrote in Ephesians 4:3 to make every effort to stay united in the Spirit and to bind ourselves together with peace. Romans 14:10 tells us to not waste our time deciding if a person is right before God or not and to 'tend to your [own] knitting.' Romans 14:19-21 tells us to use all our energy trying to get along, help each other by using encouraging words, be sensitive and courteous and don't eat, say or do things that interfere with the free exchange of love.

I'm not deluded enough to think that my old friends could welcome me back and everything would be sparkly bliss. When flesh and blood handles flesh and blood the only thing you are dealing with is death. Flesh is engorged with the blood of self and is capable of bending with every evil breeze that gusts from every corner of the imagination. A woman is not expected to take in her arms the other woman who betrayed her. However, our true identity is not found in our sin engorged flesh. We are not what we've done.

We are spiritual beings who are supposed to turn from the instinct that runs through our veins. We are supposed to deny our impulses. If a believer is filled with the spirit of God, then we all have the same spirit within us. When we, as spiritual beings, embrace another spiritual being we are actually embracing God. Because what you do to the least of men you do to Him (Matthew 25:45).

If God's spirit is within each of us and we do not belong to ourselves, then what right do we have to cut off the free exchange of love between human vessels? When you draw a line saying this is my side and this is yours, cutting some people out of your life while asking others to show where their loyalty lies, then you are not trying to get along. You cannot dice up the Heavenly father like one would dice up a tomato to toss in a salad. He is whole, He makes us whole and our denial of that is a message sent to the Father, not to the offender.

I think that it was so important in the Bible for us to use all of our energy to stay united because of what Jesus says in Mark 3:22, 'A constantly squabbling family disintegrates.' Satan ties us up in our arguments with each other in hurt feelings and need for justice. It's the 'divide and conquer' trick. Ecclesiastes 4:12 says, 'By yourself you're unprotected. With a friend you can face the worst. Can you round up a third? A three-stranded rope isn't easily snapped.' When we're divided and tied up by our disagreements, then we are effortlessly destroyed and robbed blind.

So what are you supposed to do if you have a legitimate complaint against a brother? What if he treats you unfairly and steals from you? 'If someone slaps you in the face, stand there and take it. If someone grabs your

shirt, gift-wrap your best coat and make a present of it.'
(Luke 6:29)

Forgiveness is probably the most powerful weapon for extinguishing the fire of evil intentions. The destruction stops at the point of love. Forgiveness is not only a denial of the impulse of your own flesh it's also the denial of the intents of another's flesh. It's the ultimate middle finger to the very entity of evil.

chapter ten
dusty religion

"These people make a big show of saying the right thing, but their heart isn't in it. They act like they are worshiping me, but they don't mean it. They just use me as a cover for teaching whatever suits their fancy." - Mark 7:7

I was twenty-two and had been a believer for three years when I got married and moved to live on the East Coast. For the six years of my marriage I moved around the country and never became at home in a church. At home I read the Bible and several books on religion and theology and I was able to feed my constant hunger for God and Truth. I had a lot of time to take care of my family, read and journal and that's pretty much all I did. Actually, that's pretty much all I still do.

After a while I started noticing a big difference in the preaching at church and the insight I got from my own studies. At church I was hearing a lot of the same things over and over with no growth or depth. For those first three years of my marriage I struggled with the way it sounded to call myself a Christian, but not have a church home. I was learning more from God directly than I ever did in the church, but I still wondered if something was wrong with my spiritual life since I didn't feel at home in the pew.

I would go to church because I wanted to be the complete package, but as I sat there listening to the watered down sermons, I questioned my reasons for going. I wasn't getting anything out of it nor was there opportunity for me to give anything to it. I was just another body in the pew. I decided to not try to do what I thought was expected of me and spend time with God.

The more my relationship with God grew the less connection I felt to the church 'machine'. I had a hard time finding people who could carry on a conversation about the deep truths I was learning from the Bible. Some of the mysteries of scripture were starting to make sense to me but I didn't find anyone who even thought about it as much as I do. It was either something they did on Sunday or church was a morally healthy social outlet.

I began to notice that the sermons were mainly focused on how to witness to others, how to manage your money, encouragement to not be afraid to make a bold Christian statement or how to apply a step-by-step strategy to live successfully. These things are fillers, niceties and encouragement, but they are not challenging. Those six years were a 'wilderness' for me and where my only companion was Jesus. I embraced that. What I became aware of during that 'wilderness' was like being used to the smell of fresh strawberries as you slice them versus going to out and smelling some strawberry scented lipgloss from the drug store. In one hand you have the genuine article and in the other you have the reproduction.

If you're not warping people's minds with the knowledge of who God is and what Jesus' life, death and resurrection actually means for people, then what is the point? It seems like church leaders are more interested in the numbers than they are about whether the people those numbers represent have a real relationship with God and church members are more interested in fitting in and being seen as good Christians than they are about truly knowing who God is.

If a church leader does focus more on the relationship his church has with God than how many church members he has, then the business side of things suffers and he has to start spinning his messages to increase his numbers and meet his quota. He is torn between preaching what matters and doing the things required to keep his job. He is tap dancing to a tune that has no heavenly harmony and most either give up because they can't actually do what they were called to do or they conform to the lukewarm God-spit that tries to please everybody.

⌒─❦❧❦─⌒

A lot of churches serve as a house of custom built structure that encourages conformity and tradition. They will say that everyone is welcome and after they get you in the doors then they begin to encourage you change things in your life that don't measure up to what they have decided is the right way to live.

It's like a bad boyfriend. You're out with your friends one night and meet this great guy who convinces you to go on a first date. A couple months into the relationship he starts chipping away at you. Do you have to wear so much makeup? I don't think your friends are a good influence on you. I don't think you should be wearing that shirt. You're confused. You've always worn your makeup like this, your friends are the reason you two met and you were wearing that shirt the night he asked you out.

You were good enough then, why do you have to change everything now? Does he want you for you or does he want some ideal that he's trying to mold you into? In this relationship you have two choices. You can let him chip away at you until you are no longer a person, but a robot or you can get out of the relationship.

Other churches try to utilize the emotional connections of people and they create a group that has an insatiable hunger for signs and sensations. These are not knowledge of God or proof that He exists. They are bizarre reenactments trying to recreate moments.

If you care about what they think of you and you want to be accepted, then you learn how to play the game. I don't think most people actually know that's what they're doing. They're choosing to live right, making personal sacrifices and talking the good talk. You don't notice anything is amiss because everybody looks and acts exactly the same. But who is it that tells them what is right? Are they making personal sacrifices because the hurt makes it feel more real? If you can get by being the 'good guy' long enough, then you'll start to forget that you are simply living a moral life and don't have a relationship with Jesus.

When the time comes that you need real answers and real truth and you need to be there to give the reality of God's love to someone what are you going to do? You'll come up short and then blame them because your stock phrases and Sunday school themes didn't work. A person who chooses to be authentic and refuses to use sheer will to get closer to God doesn't respond to watered down church clichés. He needs something real.

Other churches try to utilize the emotional con-

You can tell a child to stay away from the hot oven. You can explain that it's hot and it will hurt. You

can redirect him if he get curious and discipline him if he gets too close. The first kid may listen to you and not go near the oven. When the mother says no, she doesn't ask questions, she obeys. Another kid comes along and talks about wanting to touch the oven and the first kid says no, we don't touch ovens. The second kid asks why and the first kid recites what she was told. It's hot and it will hurt.

The second kid isn't convinced so he saunters over to the oven. He's a bit excited because he wants to know what the fuss is all about. What's the big deal? How hot can it be? His bath water has been too hot before and he came out fine, a bit pink but still fine. He inches toward the oven and his mom gives him a warning. He pauses and waits for her to forget about him and he begins to inch closer. She takes him to the other room and gives him a squeaky toy. He almost scoffs at the lame attempted diversion and heads toward the oven again. Soon he is scooped up, firmly swatted and placed back in the other room. He rubs his stinging rear end and decides that avoiding the disappointment of his mother and getting disciplined were more important than touching the hot oven.

When child number three comes along she is a handful. She's defiant and all over the place. When she was caught talking about wanting to touch the oven, the first kid said she couldn't. When she said she could if she wanted the second kid told her that Mother would be disappointed, so she shouldn't. When she asks why not, they both recited together what they heard. It's hot and it will hurt. She wants to know how hot. They don't know. They've never touched it. Well, then, how do they know it's true if they've never touched it? They can't answer her, they tell her that they just believe it, besides, it's better to be safe than to be sorry.

She realizes that she is not communicating with

an informed pair, she wants to touch it and she's not the type to not question things like the first child and she's not the type that will do things to make others happy, like the second child. She is determined to find the truth. She sees her opportunity and takes it. Her hand reaches for the oven with defiance and a driving need to know the truth.

In an instant, she knew what no one else was able to tell her. She found out what the truth was immediately and she continued to have that truth pounded into her memory as the pain seared it into every screaming nerve in her body. When the fourth kid comes along and starts to talk about wanting to touch the oven which of the other three children will have the bigger impact on the fourth child? Sometimes we have to fail before we can be of any use to anyone.

⚜

The guy who makes an informed decision to not know God is better off than the guy who doesn't know God, but charades as though he does. What I see in the outsider is honesty and a commitment to not be what he is not. I want to talk to the outsiders because if they genuinely want the Truth, no matter what it ended up being, then we can have some great conversations. When I talk to insiders they try to box God up and they have no depth or knowledge. It's as though I'm not talking to 'them', the person, I'm talking to 'them' the product. That's at least one reason why outsiders see them as one-dimensional.

⚜

There are a lot of different reasons for a person to start going to church and few of them have any real spiritual meaning. You could go because your mom wants you to, because a friend of yours is in a play or even because you want to add that moral 'something' to your search for meaning in life.

Going to church for the first time has got to be pretty interesting. You have to dress up in outfits that your mom would have picked out. Then you search for the Bible your grandma gave you when you were twelve. You start your car and are greeted by the Sunday morning Top Forty Countdown. You sing the tail end of number thirty-three on the countdown and when thirty-two (a song you don't particularly care for) starts in and you decide to change the station over to the Christian broadcast in honor of 'the Sabbath'. You try to get in to the song but get distracted figuring out if it's really a song or some terribly produced vacation package commercial they've been playing since the nineties.

You shut off the radio and pull in to church. It's like walking in to Wal-Mart with the greeters, flyers and offers to be of help. You find yourself saying things like, "the clear traffic was a real blessing this morning," and "it was nice fellowshipping with you." You get a few handshakes, flashes of teeth appearing from behind lips caked with lipstick and the smell of old lady. It all kind of reminds you of this late night documentary you saw on Mary Kay Conventions and you wonder if everybody is on Prozac.

After it's over, the Johnson's, a family your parents know, spot you. They invite you out for a little 'Mexicano Fiesta para libre.' Unable to turn down a free meal and a little weak in the 'no' department you agree. There was a suspicious amount of chatting about their college student who happens to be sitting directly across from you and in the middle of your enchiladas rancheras it occurs to you that they may have lured you with free food only to set you up with their not-so-bad-looking offspring. After a not horrible first date you realize that you're probably going to have to keep going to church to stay on the parent's good side.

Your reasons for going in the first place have nothing to do with an actual relationship with Jesus and your motives for continuing are even less spiritual. It's not uncommon for a 'good guy' to get plunged into leadership positions based primarily on personality and longevity. Most people can get by on performance for quite a long time. However, a situation where they need a real relationship with Jesus is when they become an absolute hindrance in the most important aspect of Christianity.

Often times, people get put into leadership positions based on circumstances other than their actual relationship with God. Getting 'involved' in church is as much a religious requirement as attending church. Most people are pressured into positions because it's another sign that their 'heart is right.' You become of a 'servant' because that's one of the pieces of religious flair that people are looking for.

Your personality gets you elected to be the youth leader at church. You know you're unqualified but, since it comes off as 'humility', it makes you an even more perfect candidate. Besides, you wonder how hard it could be to teach a Sunday school class of middle school kids. You simply say the same things you've been hearing from the other people and 'ta-da' class dismissed.

About a year later you've gotten good. The kids like you and you've been taking them out for extra stuff, like, camping trips and Christian rock concerts. You're finally married and the two of you invest all of your free time in the 'youth' at the church. You get passionate about teaching them the 'important' things in a Christian's life, like, witnessing to their friends, dressing modestly and cutting out rock and roll, not just on Sunday's but, every day. 'Treat every day like it's a Sunday.'

The tighter you pull the reins the more affirmation you get from the parents. The kids like you and want to please you so they listen to you. You've formed this fun club and they want to be included. If a new kid comes in to the mix he quickly learns that he has to conform to the dress code and the language if he wants to fit in. You've sort of become a hero with the adults in the church and they think you're amazing, a born leader.

It never occurs to you that you've merely made this a lifestyle. You've learned the language and you wear the costume and you even get a job working for a Christian organization but there is no relationship with Jesus and there is no real knowledge of God. When someone does something against the rules you modify their behavior. When they have questions about God you repeat what you've heard.

The more controlled you are in your rule keeping, the more extreme you are in your praying, the more sweat you produce and voice you lose when you're preaching, then the more you appear 'on fire' and 'sold out.' It's a lifestyle of emotional stimulation, behavior modification and solid answer evasion. Real questions about God are whisked away with answers like, "His ways are mysterious" and "I have a peace about this in my heart."

What happens when someone in your group sins? What if he does something so over the top wrong that it almost scares you? Do you doubt that he was a sincere Christian, because, after all, Christians wouldn't do that? What if he felt your disappointment and dreaded coming to church? When he finally musters up the courage, he walks in and everybody either ignores him or stares at him because they don't know how to respond. He scans the room for a friendly face, instead he sees somebody whispering because they have to explain to the person sitting next to them what happened.

He sits in the back by himself and builds up a little defensive posture and maybe even a scowl so that he can keep himself from crying in front of them. Then in an attempt to convince himself that he doesn't care what they think of him he starts acting out and wearing whatever he wants and listening to whatever he wants. He's a 'rebel' and all of his former friends think he's lost and going to Hell. They don't invite him to their parties, don't sit by him and for all intents and purposes they act like he was never part of their club.

At some point when he's able to make his own choices about whether he goes to church or not, he decides to not go. After all, why would he want to subject himself to being an outcast when he doesn't have to? He finds new friends and gets an emotional release out of making fun of 'Christians.' It eases his hurt feelings to strike out at them and since they won't let him in their club, he finds all the reasons why he would never want to anyway.

If that group had any kind of working knowledge of who God is or taught less behavior lessons and more love lessons, then the standard wouldn't be what a person does, the standard would be how a person loves. They would be trying to outdo themselves showing love and not trying to outdo themselves maintaining a standard of appearance.

If, at the very least, this kid who became the church 'outcast' by his sin had any depth of a real relationship with Jesus then, when he walked away, he would miss Him. He, in spite of the condemnation he received from his friends, would stick to his faith anyway. He would fight through the flying rocks of judgment and the death blows of hurt and anger and he would discover what the cross actually means; that, though he did something wrong, he was still wanted and loved. He would experience forgiveness with no hesitation and the life giving power from that sort of love would change him.

It would make him a better person and now that he experienced the contrast of the club member's version of Christian living and the simple love of Jesus as being the identifying factor of Christian living, he could now go back and tell them about it. He could bring life and a fresh perspective to the stagnant air of the tradition that they created. He could open a window letting in light to reveal the dust gathered on Truths that were overlooked, watered down or taken for granted. He could show them the authentic thing rather than regurgitate somebody else's version of Jesus' forgiving love.

He would be the guy who saw his friend do something stupid and he would know what to say to keep him from feeling rejected by the church. He'd tell him about the time he failed and how horrible it felt and how he learned who Jesus was in that moment of failure. Instead of turning away a life as though it were already dead, he'd be saving a life with his love.

❧ ✲✿✲ ❧

For the most part, church denominations come from the same roots and then they branch off into the more specifics. One church can require women to wear hats in the sanctuary, where another would find hats a distraction. One church allows its members to wave flags and dance in the front of the congregation where another would find it inappropriate.

The church founders are the individuals who set the tone for that particular church. Personal growth and spiritual revelation of the leaders determine what that church will major on. Where you live in the world and the personal experience of your leaders determines the details of what right living looks like in your church. This is why a person can usually shop the church flavors in their town and find a relatively comfortable fit.

Most churches are planted as a result of a spiritual revelation that their interpretation of the Bible is closer to what they believe to be the real meaning and intent. They sit down to articulate their vision for what makes their church different, doing the best they know how to put the inexplicable into words so that they can share their vision and give meaning and justification to their organization. At the moment of the birth of this new revelation it's a given that God can't be contained, that faith can't be explained and that is where worship and awe come from.

However, after years and years of celebrating the same becomes tradition. It becomes a problem when the church members decide that their church is the only way. It becomes their god in essence and if any one questions it, it frightens people, if any one rejects it, they are in effect, rejecting God and the result is they themselves getting rejected by the church members.

Leo Tolstoy in his book, 'The Kingdom of God is Within You', put it this way: "...-I believe in so and so, and so and so, and so and so to the end – to the one holy, Apostolic Church, which means the infallibility of those persons who call themselves the Church. So that it all amounts to a man no longer believing in God nor Christ, as they are revealed to him, but believing in what the Church orders him to believe in."

As creatures of habit, lovers of comfort and fear of getting off track the mold is set and new ideas and Biblical interpretations that push the envelope are viewed as being near heresy. People don't like it when their beliefs are challenged because nobody wants to think that they could be wrong.

At the same time church groups can sit around for years and say that changes need to be made but nobody ever does anything about it. They go to the front door of change and sit on the porch but never go in. The problem is that they think simply having new ideas are proof that they're progressive but talk is dead without action. Their self-satisfaction is their downfall because a person doesn't go where they think they already are.

Since when do we understand an indefinable God well enough to obnoxiously proclaim the mind of Christ with infallible certainty? God is not like us. Longevity as a Christian doesn't make you an expert on His thoughts. When He says that His ways are above ours and that His thoughts are above ours, He means just that. Unbearable familiarity and sanctimonious discernment have made the Lion of Judah into a declawed kitten.

chapter eleven
believe it or not

"What God did in this case made it perfectly plain that his purpose
is not a hit-or-miss thing dependent on what we do or don't do, but
a sure thing determined by his decision, flowing steadily from his
initiative." – Romans 9:11

God has a plan. I've heard that my whole life. Even people who don't have a relationship with Jesus say that God has a plan. If you believe that God is who He says He is then you can be sure that His plan is perfect, as is.

When things go a different direction than you expected, when you get hurt or hurt someone, when something comes up missing or dies or gets lost it is normal and human to say that it's not in God's plan, or that someone is going against God's plan. After the situation begins to clear up and you start to see good come out of it, then you call it God's plan B or C, etc. What you think is intended for evil, God used to bring about His good (Genesis 50:20). The beauty from the ashes (Isaiah 61:3) was already there. You just didn't see it right away.

God's control is not limited to your understanding of Him. When people tell you to submit yourself to Him and stop trying to control your life, it's not because you are actually keeping yourself out of His reach or effectively controlling your life. He has control whether you give it to Him or not, it's your perception of control that you have to give up.

You cannot form anything in your life unless God has it formed in your story. Psalms 139:16 (CEV) says, "Even before I was born, you had written in your book everything I would do." Your life is already written, if you try to build something that doesn't exist in your story, it won't be built. Or, as Psalms 127:1 says, "Unless the Lord builds the house, its builders labor in vain."

If you haven't submitted yourself or given up control, then don't think that you have gone where God did not intend. If you are running in the wrong direction, you're spinning your wheels, not actually going somewhere. Surrendering yourself and relinquishing control are, simply, you mentally giving in to the already active control of God.

You may want to argue that a non-Christian has driven her own life down the wrong path, come to a point of recognizing that fact and gave her life to God so that God could re-route her on to a different path of life. You may argue further that up until the point of becoming a follower of Christ, she was in control of her own life. Though she may not be aware of it, her will is secondary to God's will. She makes her choices, as God already knows the choices she'll make. She may not be aware of it, but it doesn't make it less true.

Romans 9:30 says, "Those who didn't seem interested in what God was doing actually embraced what He was doing as He straightened out their lives." There are two perspectives here. The first is human and the second is God's.

I'll describe the perspectives like I'm talking about a book. You, the reader, and she, the character, only know the story up until the page you are on. Let's say her story is 100 pages long, it's in first person and you're on page 23. Up until page 23 you see that she has exerted her will all the way down a path with no regard to anything other than her own concern.

However, in the middle of page 23 she comes to a point where she discovers the 'Rock' in the middle of her path (Romans 9:33). She becomes a believer at that point and she takes a turn off the path toward death and on to the path that leads to life.

You get to page 100 thinking you know the whole story only to discover that there is an entire other story written in between the lines and it's written upside down. You flip the book over and this time, when you read her story it's in third person. Third person is so much more informative because you have access to the author's perspective. Instead of reading a first person account that says:

I closed my eyes as I brought the flower I just picked up to my nose. I should have stopped walking, but I only shut my eyes for a moment when I tripped on a big rock and went sprawling. As I sat there with bloody shins picking tiny rocks out of my knee, I remembered the last time this happened. I was about seven years old when I fell off my bike at my grandmother's house. I was crying so hard because I was scared of how bad it would hurt to have her clean my wounds. She patiently sat there with a warm washcloth and used soft, slow strokes to get the blood off of my cuts. While she gently picked the rocks out of my knees and cleaned my scraped palms she sang "Jesus Loves Me" in such a way that soothed like only a Grandma can.

As I sit here now, I remember the feeling that came over me while she sang. We weren't a religious family, by any means, but there was something about hearing my grandma sing, "Yes, Jesus loves me, yes, Jesus loves me" that felt like a warm blanket wrap around me and take my fear away.

Not long after that my grandma died and for months I would sing her song to myself until I fell asleep. I felt like it somehow connected me to wherever she was. Sitting here now I realize it's been years since I've even thought about that time in my life. It's so odd to be brought back to that place now.

I started to hum aloud, testing it out. I felt silly at first, but kept going. Yeah, that song still had the ability to give me that warm feeling. I was brought right back to being the little girl at Grandma's knees. Where did that innocence go and how long has this longing and hollow sadness been here? I need to take some time off and figure my life out. Maybe I'll take a week and go back home...

Third person would read like this:

She is someone who appreciates the rare beauty in nature, but rarely takes the time to notice. God knew she would be taking this path for her morning run, so He grew a patch of bright white tulips (her favorite) right next to the running trail. When she nears the end of her run and has sorted out all of the mental tangles, her mind will be clearer and she will have grown used to the monotonous look of the path. She'll 'happen' upon her flowers and won't feel bad about stopping to pick them, especially when she realizes that these are the perfect replacement for the half wilted flowers in her vase at home. She closes her eyes when she smells things. It's something she's done since she was a kid. She consciously removes one *sense so that another can be stronger. Something that she hasn't done since she was a kid was fall. Hard. It will hurt her and it will slow her down for a while, but she needs to remember. She needs to remember the warmth of Gods touch because it's now time for her eyes to be open. He wants to show her why she's here.*

The almighty and omniscient Father has one plan. It's the same plan in the hard times as in the easy times. You couldn't see the good through the chaos because of your finite mind, but it doesn't mean it wasn't there.

If you can mess up God's plan with your actions and force Him to go to Plan B, C, etc. then who has the power? By definition, sovereign means possessed of supreme power and one that exercises supreme authority, an acknowledged leader; coming before all others in importance and not being under the rule or control of another. Who is sovereign, you or God?

When we have a better understanding of who God is we are no longer focused on ourselves or on the actions of others in their present form. We no longer see others or ourselves as mere sinners, righteous saints or helpless victims.

Self-awareness breeds sin simply because if the spotlight is on you then it is not on God. Losing your focus on God causes you to miss the bigger picture because your mind is on the here and the now. Seeing only present circumstances causes fear, worry and a sense of helplessness and those bring you full circle to focus on self and the cycle continues.

Self-awareness will have you trying to gain control of your present situation. You see the fear, worry etc. and recognize that they aren't Godly characteristics so you say the situation isn't in God's plan. You proclaim authority over the cosmos based on your emotional reaction to the circumstance. Your perspective is what is wrong. If you have lost your perspective on God, then you are not aware of His omniscience and you make the mistake of treating God like He doesn't know what He's doing or that He has lost control due to someone else's bad choices.

If you are continuing to ask God to reveal His will then you have lost touch with the Truth that His will already IS. You are focused on self when you begin to be your own creator. You ask God what His will is so that you can start carving out your interpretation. As a child of God you already ARE and the changes and transformations that need to take place in your life come and only by your faith in who God is do you see that there is purpose in everything. Your focus on God leaves no room for you to be worried about the happenings and people around you. That is for God to work out.

Faith in the sovereignty of God removes fear and worry. It also removes self-righteousness and pride. If God is sovereign then you can be sure that all things will be made right. You can also be sure that it is God who is doing the good that you see coming out of your own life. The good that you do is only a result of the spiritual vision that God has given you for that particular situation. The only way that you can accept credit for the holy living that you have displayed is if you have done so by method of self-control and you don't have to know God to be able to do that.

It's not uncommon for a believer to tell another not to worry about his circumstances. They say that God is in control and you can't make something happen. Only if God wants it to happen, will it happen. God's truths are not limited to the positive experiences of a believer. His truth permeates His entire creation. Nothing happens apart from God's say so whether it's in the religious realm or not.

I was asked once if I believed that it was God's will for me to have an affair with Justin. I believe that His will is bigger than that. There are many things I may never know about His purposes in this. What I do know is that it is God's will for me to know Him more completely and He used my failure to teach me these things. It wouldn't be possible for me to have the perspective that I have if I hadn't failed. I would have no reason to question anything if everything was going great. God didn't say, "Serena, I will for you to fail at the hands of Satan." He said, through Luke 22, "Serena, I've given Satan my permission to attack you and, as a result, you will fail." Some changes needed to be made and this is how He chose to bring them about.

It's the same idea as asking God if it was His will that a Roman soldier be so blind to Truth that he murders the son of God. God's will is bigger than that. It was God's will that we know Him and He used Satan's influence and human nature to bring it about.

If you don't already know that God's will is for you to know Him, then you will get caught up on the millions of things that God is using to lead you to that knowledge and you might even reject them as being outside of God's will because it doesn't fit your preconceived idea of Him and how He runs things.

When you deny the pain, you deny the discovery of God in the pain. If God wants you to know Him and He's using your sorrow to reveal Himself, then even if you shut that part of yourself off, He'll still be there waiting for you to see Him when the pain creeps back up. When you shut it out or deny it, you are also shutting out and denying Him in it. One day, when you've had enough, you'll finally hear His voice and you'll be changed through it.

You can plan all you want, 'but the Lord determines your steps' (Proverbs 16:9) and it's His 'purpose that prevails' (Proverbs 19:21). Sometimes we get a nagging accusation that our own willfulness set everything into motion and we are devastated at the thought that we have ruined everything. Romans 9:11 says, "What God did in this case made it perfectly plain that his purpose is not a hit-or-miss thing dependent on what we do or don't do, but a sure thing determined by his decision, flowing steadily from his initiative." So we can rest in peace that we are exactly where we're supposed to be. Not by our design or will, but by God's. If a season has ended, it's because it was supposed to.

You can't cancel out God's will or nullify His plan. "God's decision, His say is final." (Romans 9:13) 'Everything God wants to do in and through me, will be done (Philippians 1:19). God says, Himself, through Isaiah in chapter 46:11, 'What I have said, that I will bring about; what I have planned, that I will do. The Lord works out everything to His own ends.'

God's sovereignty not only covers finding hope in the bad times but it also covers people who think that they are achieving righteous success on their own. It's not the person, but God working in the person that does anything. We have a human nature that can make choices. There is Satan who can entice us to make certain choices and there is God who has a plan, absolute power and sight, hindsight and foresight to use both those things to carry out His will.

"But by the Grace of God there go I." That means that it is God's choosing that lets us go or keeps us. He doesn't make us do wrong and He doesn't make us do right. He initiates an action already knowing how you will respond to it and your already known response is played in His purpose.

Your circumstances are no accident. When you

have failed, when someone has hurt you, when things are falling apart or if your seat right now is not a good one and you don't understand what's going on, then try to remember that you are learning and growing and God is going to bring something good out of where you are that He couldn't have without what's happening. Our perspective is limited to the right now and there is a lot that we are blind to. We are small and God is very big and things like this remind us of that. Your faith in the identity of God can get you through times like this if you have a clear understanding of who God is in the first place.

He promises to work all things out for the good of those who believe in Him. Knowing that and believing it can give you an amazing freedom and peace. The kind of peace that you don't have any real tangible reason for having other than your belief that God is who He says He is.

I heard a sermon on the radio talking about applying the strategies of David to defeat the 'Goliaths' in our lives. That should have been the shortest sermon ever because David didn't have a 'strategy.' He simply had a better understanding of who God was than the other people around him. He knew that if God wanted Goliath to be defeated then David could have flicked the giant with his finger and he would have fallen over dead. David chose to use a weapon he was used to and he slung a rock at him. It's not a strategy or formula, it was his belief.

What would you say to a person who you were trying to convert to Christianity? You'd tell him that the requirement for salvation is to believe that Jesus is the son of the one true God and you'd probably quote John 3:16.

Have you ever noticed that witnessing tracks are small pieces of paper explaining that Jesus paid the price for their sin and that by believing that simple truth they are 'in'? What a contrast to the millions of book pages that tell them how to maintain that salvation. "Let me put this question to you: How did your new life begin? Was it by working your heads off to please God? Or was it by responding to God's Message to you? Are you going to continue this craziness? For only crazy people would think they could complete by their own efforts what was begun by God. If you weren't smart enough or strong enough to begin it, how do you suppose you could perfect it?" (Galatians 3:2-4)

In the religious world you will find an abundant amount of strategies and formulas that address the day to day practices of a church attendee. Some of the most popular books out there right now put Christian living into a tangible multi-step program. This sort of teaching gets away from the infinite that is so hard to grasp and introduces a more finite theology that is easier to cling to. It helps them manage and control themselves. They are so popular because they produce an attainable and applicable structure.

Strategies, formulas, don'ts and to-do lists are all focused on behavior modification. What is so dangerous about that is a person doesn't have to have a relationship with God to apply these practices. If a person gets the steps down then, by all appearances, they are living a successful life built on Christian standards. If they are practicing the Christian moral code and have no spiritual wisdom, then what keeps them from overstepping their boundaries as brother in Christ into the more often seen self-righteous god complex? If you are maintaining your appearance by pure sweat and self-control, then no wonder you are abusive to others who aren't as disciplined as you.

We like to have all the answers and there are too many questions that go unanswered when you start talking in plain language instead of watered down clichés from the church. There are too many things that can't be explained.

It's hard to imagine a God that isn't always joy, laughter, sunshine and full bellies. It's hard to imagine a God within the dark so we only focus on God in the light. We only give credit to God when it's peace and joy that we see.

Some of the reasons that we don't have a right view of God or His activity are because our main focus is to convert as many people as possible to Christianity. If we were to tell a person who recently went through a tragedy that God allowed it in their lives, how would it make that person feel toward God? It's too big of a risk. You don't want people to be angry with God.

When you don't acknowledge the fullness of whom God is then you leave huge holes in the faith system. It's as though you need to protect Him from the opinions of others if they were to know how far He would go to show that He is God. You have this need to protect His unconventional ways from a people that think He should be more docile. You only talk about His blessings and His rewards to righteous living and personal sacrifice. If something goes wrong in another person's life you either don't have an answer or you blame them. Saying it's because they are out of the 'river', out of His light, off His path, out of His will or diverted from His plan.

Why don't you believe the Bible when it says that your will is secondary to His or when it says that He is in complete control over everything? Why do you give Satan or other human beings so much credit for the things as though God's hands were tied? My answer is simple. It requires too much faith.

It requires too much faith to believe that God is in control when your life feels so out of control. It requires too much faith to think that the calamity you find yourself in could possibly be part of God's plan for your life. It requires too much faith in the God, whom you know is good, to have any part of what doesn't feel good. You have preconceived ideas that, if it were God's way, then there would be no pain and no failure. It requires too much faith to believe that God would use both pain and failure to bring you to discover Him. That is, unless He already has. Accepting or rejecting doesn't change the Truth. It changes you.

chapter twelve
the problem with being alive

"Now if I do what I do not want to do, it is no longer I who do it,
but it is sin living in me that does it."
- Romans 7:20

It's hard to imagine a bigger problem in the church than keeping up appearances. Those who are on the church payroll recognize the demands. The pressure to be the person that everyone expects is intense and it doesn't just fall on his shoulders. Any person that he has a relationship with has to measure up as well. Very few have the courage to disregard the expectations and be authentic. Most choreograph their lives to the graceless ballet of legalism drenched in self-importance.

There are few differences between his job and the job of a politician. His survival and livelihood has entirely to do with public approval. His paycheck comes from donations from church members. He puts on his best suit, smiles at the grandmas, kisses the babies and talks about golf with the men. He stands in front of the congregation and explains why his job is necessary and it's not uncommon for him to balloon his stories in order to have greater appeal to the emotions of the possible donors.

He becomes a slave to his appearance. He keeps secrets, avoids restaurants with bars and makes a point to publicly boycott certain people, places and things so that everyone can see how pure he is. If someone close to him messes up he makes a public example of them and disassociates himself. He has built a life of public approval filled with pats on the back and money slipped in to handshakes.

At no time does it occur to him that he has become a product of debauchery and he cannot get through to a single life that needs Jesus. He uses his personal appeal as his attraction and skates by on the thin ice of public approval. His survival is dependent on appearing blameless and he will not hesitate to destroy another human character in order to make any comparison between them and himself a matter of arrogant sneer. Does anyone notice how quickly his mouth moves in his jittery performance as he vomits slandering death decrees on those who could reveal his true character? Who would contradict such a vigorous cabaret if the contradiction would have them smeared in sludge along with the other hapless target?

If more people knew the truth about what is actually important in the life of a follower of Jesus, then the casualties of the church 'country club' society would be the minority. We've developed a system of classes in professional Christianity where the more self-sacrificial and glossy you appear the more power and approval you collect.

We talk about a person's sparkling personality, their witty sense of humor and delightful disposition and never give thought to the roadblocks that these things put in the way of the message of redemption. The allure is one of persona that is in the realm of self and the desired 'harvest' is lured to a man of flesh and blood who offers nothing but an opinionated example of how a Christian life should appear. That only leads to a refined religious lifestyle.

Operating under the realm of self is the opposite of operating under the realm of God and their teaching supports self accomplishment. If your message orbits around you, then it obviously does not have God at the center. Your message may sell, but it won't ever save.

The message that does save is the one that teaches Jesus as the son of God who became a man so that he could die the sinner's death and save every single person who ever lived from their inevitable fate. When you're in your Sunday school class teaching a group of high school students about the proper way to dress, maybe you could ask yourself what role their appearance plays in saving their life.

When a person is in a relationship with Jesus those things work themselves out in their own time. It isn't for us to fabricate the external culture of a relationship with Jesus thereby cheapening the effects of a life in union with God. What a horribly misguided sense of purpose. Do you not know that developing a list of rules antagonizes the resting rebellion that sleeps beneath our skin?

The law breeds sin. It entices, seduces and dares sin. Romans 7:5 says, "...the sinful passions aroused by the law were at work in our bodies so that we bore fruit for death." The law was written out so that we wouldn't have to guess at how to live a moral life. A few verses later, Paul explains, "The law code started out as an excellent piece of work. What happened, though, was that sin found a way to pervert the command into a temptation, making a piece of 'forbidden fruit' out of it. The law code, instead of being used to guide me, was used to seduce me... The very command that was supposed to guide me into life was cleverly used to trip me up, throwing me headlong."

In this crippling cycle of trying to live by a code that only point out your shortcomings, your focus is, no doubt, on yourself in relation to the law. The law has the power in that situation. In your most violent effort to live up to the expectation, to not fail, you are absolutely failing. It is gut wrenching to think about, but look at it. You are focused on and living for the law. So, when you come to the part of the law code where it says you are to have no other god's before Him, there is the crushing realization that in trying to be right, you have become wrong.

Nobody can be trusted completely to make their own decisions as to what is right and wrong. It has to be spelled out for us. Yet, knowing the rules doesn't give you the power to follow them. You can want to do the right thing and still end up doing the wrong thing. The war inside of you keeps you from gaining complete control of yourself and Paul says a bit later that the power of sin inside the person keeps sabotaging their best intentions.

So now we understand the need for a savior. God wants to have a relationship with His creation. That relationship is dependent on your 'rightness,' so, He paid the law off. He assumed the identity of every single offense written in the code and identified himself with every single label caused by sin and He paid the price for it. This means that the law no longer has power over you. It doesn't mean that you can live with no regard to right. It means that you are no longer held to it.

The body is a being that is entirely separate from the spirit. For example, are you still you if you lose a limb, or your eyesight? The answer is yes. The 'you' is your spirit the remainder is your body. The body has its own name with its own nature, desires and urges. When you become a believer in Jesus, his 'self' or spirit comes and lives in your body and becomes one with your true self, giving your spirit, which was once dead, life with a new name that only He knows. Now there are two completely separate natures at work in the one body, the flesh and the spirit.

The spirit of God in the body is good, but the body it inhabits is corrupt. That's why you can find yourself doing things with your body that make your insides churn with disappointment. The man can scan a restaurant for a table and find a pair of legs that make him wonder what else there is to see and then he snaps out of it wanting to punch himself for being so crude. The problem with being alive is that sin is alive in you also. If you are not your body, then you are not the one sinning, but the body is. Paul says it like this, "Now if I do what I do not want to do, it is no longer I who do it, but it is sin living in me that does it."

You can't look to your right or to your left and decide whether or not that man is a failure to his master. You are arguing about things. You are concerning yourselves with wine and music and movies and so on, when you should be concerned with what God speaks to you about you. "Forget about deciding what's right for each other. Here's what you need to be concerned about: that you don't get in the way of someone else, making life more difficult than it already is. I'm convinced—Jesus convinced me!—that everything as it is in itself is holy. We, of course, by the way we treat it or talk about it, can contaminate it." (Romans 14:13-14)

We're not supposed to sit around and discuss what is acceptable as a follower and what is unacceptable. You, in your quest to develop a picture of what you think right living should look like, most definitely are excluding lives that aren't like yours. You do not have the insight needed to determine if a life is connected to God or not. You cannot see into that individual's heart and decide that the place where they are is not the place that God is meeting them. As a matter of fact, "since you died with Christ to the basic principles of this world, why, as though you still belonged to it, do you submit to its rules: 'Do not handle! Do not taste! Do not touch!'? These are all destined to perish with use, because they are based on human commands and teachings. Such regulations indeed have an appearance of wisdom, with their self-imposed worship, their false humility and their harsh treatment of the body, but they lack any value in restraining sensual indulgence." (Colossians 2:20-23 NIV) It's not about the Do's and Don'ts, "it's what God does with your life as He sets it right, puts it together, and completes it with joy." (Romans 14:17)

Religion can't save you. You can know the ins and outs of everything in the law code, but that doesn't set you in the right. Rule keeping looks good on paper, but it doesn't have the power to save you. You could be your own savior by mere self-control if that were the case. Romans chapter two says that those who teach the law actually turn people off and make them down on God because of their inability to keep to the rules themselves.

Romans chapter three says that we have 'proved that we are utterly incapable of living the glorious lives God wills for us' yet, 'out of sheer generosity He puts us in right standing with himself. A pure gift. He got us out of the mess we're in and restored us to where He always wanted us to be. And He did it by means of Jesus Christ.'

Since there is only one God, then He is the God of the outsider as well as the insider. 'God sets right all who welcome his action and enter into it, both those who follow our religious system and those who have never heard of our religion.' When we take our eyes off of what we do and focus on what God does we don't 'cancel out all our careful keeping of the rules and ways God commanded'. In fact, we 'by putting that entire way of life in its proper place' actually 'confirm it' because lives in step with God take on the shape that was originally intended.

Romans chapter four explains how to put that way of life in its proper place. If we are able to earn God's approval by what we do, then we can take full credit for our 'right' standing. If you can earn your way by rule keeping, then your own self-satisfaction is your wage for that hard work. You can sit in your easy chair and feel content in your moral sweat. You do not get in on God's approval by what you do, but by what He does.

God does not keep score and His gift is available to everyone, not just those who keep our religious ways.

"Do you think it is possible that the blessing could be given to those who never even heard of our ways, who were never brought up in the disciplines of God? We all agree, don't we, that it is by embracing what God did for [us] that [we are] declared fit before [Him]?" (Romans 4:8-9)

"We know very well that we are not set right with God by rule-keeping but only through personal faith in Jesus Christ. How do we know? We tried it—and we had the best system of rules the world has ever seen! Convinced that no human being can please God by self-improvement, we believed in Jesus as the Messiah so that we might be set right before God by trusting in the Messiah, not by trying to be good." (Galatians 2:15-16)

"Is it not clear to you that to go back to that old rule-keeping, peer-pleasing religion would be an

abandonment of everything personal and free in my relationship with God? I refuse to do that, to repudiate God's grace. If a living relationship with God could come by rule-keeping, then Christ died unnecessarily." (Galatians 2:19)

"Answer this question: Does the God who lavishly provides you with his own presence, his Holy Spirit, working things in your lives you could never do for yourselves, does He do these things because of your strenuous moral striving or because you trust Him to do them in you? Don't these things happen among you just as they happened with Abraham? He believed God, and that act of belief was turned into a life that was right with God." (Galatians 3:5-6)

"The obvious impossibility of carrying out such a moral program should make it plain that no one can sustain a relationship with God that way. The person who lives in right relationship with God does it by embracing what God arranges for him. Doing things for God is the opposite of entering into what God does for you. Habakkuk had it right: "The person who believes God, is set right by God—and that's the real life." Rule-keeping does not naturally evolve into living by faith, but only perpetuates itself in more and more rule-keeping, a fact observed in Scripture: 'The one who does these things [rule-keeping] continues to live by them'." (Galatians 3:11-12)

What if you could have it only one way, either a person's heart is pure before God or their external appearance is a well-oiled machine of goodness? Teach them things that magnify the absolute authority of God. Be the reflection of a person who looks to God rather than to anything in the here and now. Teach them to wait for the beauty while they're in the ashes. Show them that their own sin only intensifies the awareness of their need for Jesus. Your sin speaks nothing new about your human condition.

We don't teach people to love God for what He does, but for who He is. Why would you mislead people by contradicting the very nature of God when you make them feel that they can earn God's favor by what they do and don't do rather than for being who they are? You may not think that's what you're doing, but what do you spend your time focusing on? You try to clean up your life and make it appear like a life lead by the spirit when you have no clue what the spirit even cares about at that given moment.

You tell a man that he has to stop smoking in order to be in right relationship with God, but God just wants the man to stop mentally undressing his secretary when she walks into his office. Sure, he can appease the public if he stops smoking and nobody will bat an eye at him, but what is he to do about the sin that occupies his imagination?

Matthew chapter five says that though murder is a sin, you've already committed the crime in your head with your anger before you ever did anything about it. You stand to be hauled into court by mere thoughts alone. Why is it then, that if a man stays pure in thought but sins in action he is held under deeper waters than the one who thinks it on a regular basis? A man's heart holds his intentions, isn't it clear that God judges the man's heart and not his flesh?

chapter thirteen
the bitter cup

If someone falls into sin, forgivingly restore him,
saving your critical comments for yourself.
- Galatians 6:2

To say that God is sovereign is to say that there are no accidents, no coincidence and no victims. When you find yourself in a place of pain, sorrow or suffering then you are in a place where you are not sufficient and it's hard to imagine that God would be in something that causes you to hurt. You can medicate yourself either literally or figuratively. You can deny that you are in this place, which takes quite a bit of mental manipulation. You can fill your awareness with an assortment of distractions, but until you enter the sorrow you will not grow. You will either receive yourself in suffering or be destroyed by it.

Prior to your personal end, you have an awareness of growing on your own. You may be aware of God and Him working in your life but your perception is that He is responding to you and your dealings. "God does not respond to what we do, we respond to what He does." (Romans 3:28, emphasis mine) Until you are in a place of questioning God or His existence and until you are in a place of questioning your knowledge of or devotion to God then you have not yet reached the end of yourself and the end of your self-initiated so called growth.

A person doesn't need to question any of these things if they are not in a place of turmoil. You may believe that things are falling apart in this time but God sees an opening to reveal Himself. It is only for your gain that you are allowed to suffer. A man who has not received himself through the fires of sorrow is more likely to be disapproving and pompous toward others and end up turning them away. On the other hand, those who have been through their own personal hell can be used as nourishment for other people.

Listen to the stories from people throughout history when they talk about miracles that take place and the moments that built their faith. It was when they couldn't do any more. It was in the moments where they were face to face with their humanity, be it weakness, hardness or faultiness. Their situation required what they could not produce. God stepped in to fill the inadequacy, illuminating Himself in the process and solidifying the faith of those who witnessed it.

Something we do, as part of the human condition is tie knots, build barricades and take on postures that counterfeit the spirit of God. You can look at the rest of the world to see what kind of effect this has.

Tensions, divisions and incompleteness are the result of having no Godly perspective. Disputes are prevalent, families are no longer united and there are gaping holes left in the hearts and lives of people. A follower of Christ cannot do those things. We have to forfeit our rights as human beings who are entitled to pursue personal gain. This sounds so bleak and depressing, but the story doesn't stop with us submitting ourselves.

We have to come to a place where we have lost

ourselves and have a sense of personal death. The amazingly backward way that God works is called the 'Great Reversal' in Matthew 19:28. He takes you in that precise state of nothingness, originating with surrendering your claim on your desires, and He replaces what you lost with authentic peace, spacious joy and awareness of purpose. Even bigger than that, when you give up the deed to your life, your very birthright, He replaces it with His life and His birthright.

You no longer belong to yourself. Your responsibility to better yourself or to seek your own has been handed over. You belong to God. Before you traded your old life for your new one you would have reached the end of your life and inherited what everybody inherits, a Certificate of Death. After you traded your life, you traded up, so when you reach the end of your life you inherit what children of God inherit, a Certificate of Life.

I'm not saying anything new, maybe just in a new way. These things have been said the same way over and over and we've conditioned ourselves to not even notice it anymore. It's like the person who lives next to train tracks has become so used to the jarring noise that he doesn't even wake up when it shakes his house as it goes by.

Jesus has become a brand just short of being trademarked and His words have saturated the knick-knack market. It's a market where the bubble gum sweet flavor doesn't last through the first unyielding bubble, but we chew it anyway because it's got the 'J.C.' brand. The roar of the Lion of Judah is displayed in an outdated graphic design on a bumper sticker stuck to the back of a dirty Dodge Caravan. The van pulls up to a Sunday afternoon buffet where the occupants, donning their cheap witnessing t-shirts, gorge on enough food to feed a small country then pop a scripture inscribed breath mint.

Assuming their worn out waitress is not saved, since she's working on Sunday, they decide to steal from her by leaving a fake twenty dollar bill that tells her how she can get 'saved.' She has to pay taxes on tips whether she gets them or not. If, in fact, she is not a believer, what do you think she is saying to herself as she's on all fours picking up the defiled napkins and half chewed bits of fried goodness that most likely fell out of their mouths as they were performing their well-practiced glutinous opera?

I'll return to my personal story to illustrate the devastating effects of a violent fight to regain control over a situation. This is quite possibly the hardest part of my story because it's the area that is the most damaged. It hasn't, yet, been made right. In this story there remains a hemorrhaging tear the size of a father's love for his child.

◦—❧❦—◦

On July 5, 2005, Justin took Chloe, his two-year-old daughter, to pre-school. On the way, he told her that he had to go away for a little while and that he would be back. He stood outside of her classroom for a few moments before he left. He was broken and needed to heal and he chose to do that in a place where he could find solitude, which meant that he would have to leave her with her mother. When he unlatched her car seat that Tuesday morning, he had no idea that it would be the last time.

When Anne came home from work she found the letter that Justin left. I don't know how long it took her to do what she did next. It could have been that same day or the next, but definitely within that week and a half, she removed every single photograph and item that would connect a memory to Justin from the house and she began praying that God would remove Chloe's memory of her daddy from her heart. When Chloe asked where her daddy was, Anne would tell her that he had to go away.

When Justin called home after being gone for ten days, Anne promised him that she would never do anything that would hinder a relationship between him and their daughter. He told her that he trusted her and when they ended the conversation he knew that their next step would be finalizing a divorce and setting up a visitation schedule. He never spoke to an attorney. He trusted Anne completely. After all, he was the one who did the wrong, not her.

Justin agreed to be lead by Anne's discretion simply because he believed what she said. He had no idea that while Anne told him that she would never keep him from having a relationship with Chloe, she replaced pictures of him with a picture of Jesus, which she hung on Chloe's bedroom wall. Anne would show her the picture of Jesus and tell her that it was her 'new daddy'.

Anne told him not to worry because Chloe was fine without him. Anne also told him that she put her in counseling and seeing him would damage the progress in the efforts Anne was making. While Justin trustingly waited, he asked for pictures of his daughter. A few months passed since the last time he saw her. He wasn't allowed to attend her third birthday party and his heart ached at the thought of missing out on any of her life. Anne responded with a letter denying his request because 'it wouldn't be healthy' for him to have pictures of her. He was confused and crushed, but still trusting.

Justin's brokenness in this time period made him easily manipulated. He had no self-confidence and did not believe that he was a good enough person to tell someone that they were making the wrong decision. He was in a position of absolutely prostrating himself to the woman he blind sided with his affair. He thought that appeasing her would bring him closer to being able to be a father to his daughter. It was only a matter of time to ease her fears and prove to her that he can be trusted to follow her lead.

After nearly a year of denials, Anne finally agreed to a face-to-face meeting with Justin. It was an important day for him and all morning you could hear it in his voice. He was excited because he saw this meeting as the beginning steps to reconciliation. He found out quickly that this was not the case.

When Justin asked if they could start a visitation schedule for him and Chloe, she refused. She told him that Chloe's counseling was ongoing and that she switched between several different counselors until Anne found one she believed would benefit their situation. She explained that she finally found a therapist who would give Chloe the 'tools' she needed to 'compartmentalize' this 'traumatic event' so she could separate her awareness of something that might cause her pain from the other areas of her life.

She would not disclose the name of the counselor and she refused to include him in the counseling. All contact with Justin and members of his family were to be categorically denied until further notice.

Before the conversation was over, she may have sensed his pain because she affirmed him in his ability to be a wonderful father. She wished him luck, peace and forgiveness.

As the next months went by, he continued to send letters asking to be able to see Chloe. Justin's letters annoyed Anne and she would say she was confused that he would even ask given their previous conversations. She said Chloe would be damaged if she were to see her him. Anne said Chloe was too young to understand her father's sin and he would have to wait until she was older. Nothing made sense to him, but he was not in a position to fight her. She held the control.

On August 25, 2006, Mitch posted a blog on his web site announcing his engagement to Anne. He called their upcoming marriage 'God's plan of redemption' and said they are 'thrilled' to 'accept it'. It seems that Mitch's excessive desire to appear without blemish has given him motive to extract blood from the veins of God's living Word. Not only is his view of himself vibrantly illuminated, but more importantly is the indication that such deliberate misuses of scripture go seemingly unnoticed when said the right way.

Instead of Mitch seeing God's grace as the reason he can marry Anne, he attempts to remove his need for grace by calling it something that makes him appear to be a redeemer. God's plan of redemption included sending Jesus, the Son of God, to save His people. Though Mitch has a purpose in his life and has the potential for God to use him to do many things, the plan of redemption does not include sending Mitch, the son of a writer, to save His people.

The month after Mitch and Anne were married Justin received an e-mail asking him to relinquish his parental rights and let Mitch adopt Chloe. If there was an exact moment where I witnessed a man's heart tear open wide, it was in that instant. He demanded a face-to-face meeting immediately and was asked to wait until after the New Year, which was three weeks away.

When Justin found out that Mitch was going to be part of that meeting, my heart sank at the inevitable outcome. By this time I was well aware of Mitch's remarkable talent for massaging his acrobatic scriptures. I imagined Justin sitting there in a busy restaurant across from two people who want to make him disappear. I decided I would go with him if only to be a presence of balance.

What I witnessed in that meeting was exactly what I feared. Justin went in with an open heart and would not let any fear or solid thoughts take root in his mind beforehand. He purposely went in to that meeting unrehearsed and unprepared.

Their message was rehearsed to the point of not leaving room to listen to anything other than opportunities to twist words and pound home the message. As I sat and listened to them repeat phrases like automatons I could almost hear their conversations that prepared them for that meeting. "Every time he mentions that he is her father, tell him that she doesn't feel a void. When he says that he loves her and wants to have a relationship with her, tell him that he is being selfish for wanting to damage her. When he says 'I', tell him it's not about him, it's about the child. Assure him that he's a wonderful father, but that Chloe will not remember him and feels no void in his absence."

Anne told Justin about a time when their daughter saw a picture of him at a friend's house. She asked who it was and Anne told her it was 'Justin.' This was Anne's way of proving that her efforts of removing Justin from Chloe's memory were successful.

Justin realized he was not talking to two people who are truly open to doing what is best for Chloe when Anne refused to include him in their counseling. He realized that he was talking to two people who would manipulate scripture to fit their agenda when Anne asked Justin to be like Abraham and Isaac and walk Chloe up the hill and sacrifice her. Maybe Anne doesn't remember the story of Abraham and Isaac well because when the father and his child got to the top of the hill, God provided an alternate sacrifice.

The moment Justin became fully aware that

Anne never had intentions of letting him see his daughter came when he asked Mitch if Chloe called him Daddy. I'll never forget what it was like to see my husband's entire world rip out from under him. I saw a part of Justin die. Mitch answered the question with another question, 'What do *you* think she should call me?' Time froze when Justin's almost inaudible realization slipped through his lips, 'She *does* call you Daddy.'

Anne has said over and over that she wants what is best for her child. I can understand how Anne could have a desire to never have to deal with Justin again. She would rather cut off the memory than go through the painful process of reconciliation.

❧ ✥✥✥ ☙

Denial and dissociation imitate the feelings of peace and freedom. It doesn't take much to understand that, to Anne, the prospect of letting her daughter be cared for by the two people who hurt her most would cause such negative emotion that the all-together elimination of the possibility would feel exceedingly peaceful. So, the entire emotional situation gets buried and freedom is declared. This perceived 'freedom' comes at the high price of true freedom. It's only a band-aid and it barely covers a wound that promises to never go away until it's dealt with properly. The longer you wait the less likely you'll do the right thing because the wound continues to accumulate baggage.

I couldn't help but hear the echo of Mitch's words to me regarding his ex-wife, Madeline. He told me that she needed to lose the most important thing to her because of what she had done. He spun it in such a way that clouded my judgment and he decorated his wishes with tattered pieces of scripture. As the words echoed through my memory, I wondered if he gave a similar speech to Anne regarding Chloe.

When we lose our sight of the sovereignty of God we are apt to take on our situations and do as we see best in the present circumstance. The problem with this is that our own perceived strengths become our devastating downfall. Our ability to make things right is limited by our experience in history, lack of knowledge of purpose in the present pain and blindness that leads to fear of the unknown future outcome.

Religion has the potential to be intensely damaging when a person with no Godly perspective goes about asserting authority over situations in the name of the Almighty. There is no sanction for someone who believes they are doing the will of God and some of the most damage happens when a vision impaired warrior starts slinging his sword at anything that threatens his comfort level.

In a believer's life, the only thing we are supposed to deny is ourselves. We are instructed to do so because it's our own desires that get in the way of the things that God asks of us. He asks us to love one another, to work out our differences and to go to the ends of the earth to reconcile with our brothers and sisters in Christ so that we can be whole. If you are focused on the way it makes you feel or what it costs you, then it is less likely that you will do it.

You can name a dozen reasons why you are justified in your actions, but the way you feel about a situation and being justified in it is not what is important. What is important to God is that you hand everything over to Him. Self-sacrifice is not to be mistaken with getting up early to read your Bible. I'm not saying that you shouldn't make time to read your Bible. I'm saying that sort of sacrifice leads to pride in yourself for making the sacrifice. Therefore, it's a false source of surrender. A real self-sacrifice has more to do with sacrificing your pride, justice and peace of mind for the sake of getting in on what the Spirit is doing under the surface. Self sacrifice always leads to you losing your sense of self and losing your sense of self is always uncomfortable.

Part of denying yourself is denying your need for control, inner peace, superficial happiness and comfort. These things are so difficult to give up because they require you to not only see past yourself but also to see in to eternity. We are not naturally able to do that, that's why you have to put your trust in God with no promise of personal gain and no promise that things will work the way you want them to. You have to trust Him for the sake of trusting Him.

As I said before, this is the most painful part of the story because it's the part that hasn't been made right. I'm not going to make an attempt to polish this up thereby cheapening the process that those involved will eventually go through. Chloe is loved fiercely by both of her parents. She is loved so much by her father that he refuses to rip her in half just so he can have his share. He is trusting God to reveal Himself through this.

When someone sins against you, your response to it can either cancel it out or perpetuate it. A good reason to perpetuate someone's sin is so you can marinate in their consequences and use their suffering as a healing balm for your own wounds.

If you take away your vengeance, you take away your balm. Then who is going to heal you? Who do you have that can sooth your wounds?

chapter fourteen
varnish

"They talk a good line, but they don't live it.
They don't take it into their hearts and live it out in their behavior.
It's all spit-and-polish veneer." - Matthew 23:1

I don't know how to tell you to forgive someone. I can tell you that you would be saving their life if you did, but other than that, I don't think that your desire to forgive is comparable to that person's need for it. Maybe you need to find yourself in a place where you can identify with your own need for forgiveness then it's more likely you'll be able to offer it to someone else.

I don't completely understand forgiveness. I can identify with needing it, but the awareness of my need to forgive isn't as powerful in me right now. What I feel more than anything is the potential to forgive a lot quicker than I would have been able to before this happened. People do some stupid things and it gets out of hand before you know it. I, of all people, know that.

There is nothing like the eyes of someone who has fallen and is under attack. It's like there is an unseen force dismantling them from the inside out and no medication, no mental affirmation, no person, nothing can come close to easing it. Your old friend is trapped inside going through the unspeakable and their eyes may appear dead at first, but if you look closely you'll see fear, hopelessness and torment.

Hopefully you wouldn't make the mistake that our friends made. They saw fear and hopelessness and said that those were not characteristics of Christians, so torment is part of it and they walked away. Sometimes a person is under such a forceful attack that they can't talk, but if you could hear what every cell in their body was screaming from the inside you would recognize at least two words. '*Help me.*'

Nothing would have helped me more than if someone were to find me buried deep within myself and whisper the story of Jesus into my spirit and then tell it to me over again. There was a poison in my body and my 'sorry' wasn't enough to make it go away. I couldn't take it back, though I would have given anything to.

My biggest battle was when I needed to forgive myself. I was incapable of that for a long time. It's quite a battle to have any sense of value after something like this.

⌁ ✿✿✿ ⌁

When I was reading Philippians chapter three, I came across the phrase 'cross haters' and I wondered about what would make someone hate the cross. Satan hates the cross. You would think that a non-believer would be a 'cross hater', but then you don't hate something you don't believe in. So, it's not the non-believers we have to worry about.

A cross hater is anyone who shows distaste for

what the cross stands for and the immediate access it gives to everybody regardless of their rap sheet.

Mitch told me that my failure was the same as me spitting at Jesus on the cross. My failure is what the cross was for and his accusation was an attempt to keep me from the gift of grace that Jesus died for. As though he needed to protect the cross from me, his words made me feel like I couldn't find forgiveness because my sin deemed me unworthy.

The fact that Jesus was already the price paid for me means that there is never a point where I have gone too far. Even if I were to actually spit on the cross it would soak up my saliva and I would be forgiven before I reached the back of my hand to wipe the spit off my mouth. So, who is my accuser angrier with, me or the absolute blatant injustice of the cross?

To hate the cross is to hate the entire redemption plan that it signifies. To hate the cross is to hate the One who is capable of forgiving the cross hater. You can't dodge the injustice of grace. The more you hate it, the more you need it the stronger it becomes. It's a relentless cycle of grace that cannot be escaped.

❧ ⬧⬧⬧ ☙

It's hard to deal with such grace when you don't find yourself needing it. However, in spite of the resume you have acquired in this small world, you are severely handicapped with a mental impediment which is such a barrier that it's only because of God's massive and uncontainable love that He gives you a purpose in this world at all.

Don't for a second think that you can speak anything but extravagant love, generous grace and unending mercy to anyone, ever, if you are going to claim to be speaking the mind of Christ. You are far too ignorant of the full story to risk speaking in any other way. Look at it like this, chances are stacked as high as the heavens that you will be wrong no matter how sure you feel about sizing up someone's relationship with God. Would it not be safer to be wrong showing love to someone it will not change than to write off someone whom God has chosen to lift up?

If you place yourself in opposition of someone whom God has chosen to shine His light through, then you have in effect placed yourself in opposition of God. Would you pray that the light be hidden from the public view in order to achieve your self-serving agenda to punish the unworthy 'swine' who feed off of undeserved grace? A cross hater is a grace hoarder who says that Jesus died for those who don't need it, not for those who don't deserve it.

⁓—❧❧❧—⁓

Religion, when used for selfish agenda, is possibly the most destructive force of evil. Blaise Pascal, a religious philosopher from the 1600's, said it perfectly, "Men never do evil so completely and cheerfully as when they do it from religious conviction." When someone believes that they are acting on behalf of the supreme authority they can do unthinkable harm to others. If you hear a voice in your spirit to devalue a human life and to deny unending grace and love then you are not hearing from God, you are entertaining evil.

Grace isn't an excuse to avoid the responsibility to do right. You are expected to do right, but when you fail, confess it then move on taking each day by itself and leaving it behind when it's passed. You can learn the law and follow it to the best of your human abilities, denying yourself and suffering for 'the cause', but idealistic martyrs don't get extra points on the scoreboard. If you had the power to maintain a level of sinlessness on your own, then where is your need for Christ?

No one will chastise you for your self-inflicted, sacrificial lifestyle, and that is possibly the scariest trap one could fall into. You sneak through the cracks of religion without ever having to have real relationship with Jesus. You appear right, so you must be right. You get a degree of confidence and affirmation as you receive your approving nods. Nobody suspects a thing.

Once your façade has maintained traditional approval it is pompously impossible for you to show any bit of weakness or failure. It goes against everything you've been able to visibly maintain and is terribly confusing to any of your admirers. Failure, consequently, is suffered in the dark and it is stifled and swept away but never fully eradicated. This leaves you with a lot of animosity which leaves you feeling less 'Christ-like' and the only answer to that dilemma is to tighten the grip on yourself even more.

✧─❦❧─✧

The double talk from the pulpit is predictable and the blanket phrases say nothing. They make a grab for your interest by using corny ways to identify with you. They inject you with a cocktail of guilt, fear and resolution and then pressure you to display your agreement by raising your hand or standing up in front of everyone else.

It's the same feeling as being at a time share convention where all the same tactics are used to get you to buy into an idea by manipulating your senses and emotions and pressuring you to do something about it. It's all about numbers and who is earning them. They send you off with a packet of information, get you registered and start sending you a bill of expectations.

⟡

I'm tired of hearing people talk about their 'unsaved' friends and how draining it is to be around them, but they struggle through because they are a 'witness' to them. A witness of what, exactly? If you're drained just being in their presence, then why are you there? Do you think that your randomly injected 'church talk' and influence on them is that compelling? An uptight, worn out opportunist who twists every natural friendship connection into an avenue to change them into whom you think they should be is as pleasant as an afternoon with a hungry salesman.

I've sat in a circle with other people as they talked about their non-Christian friends. It's as though they have to justify their friendship by making it an opportunity to 'introduce them to Christ.' They'll request prayer for their friend and share 'testimony' about their conversations. Through the course of listening I have learned about that friend's sexual behavior and inner thoughts that have been shared in the confidence of 'friendship.' They make comments about 'wearing her down' and 'almost got her' to track their 'witnessing' progress. I thought to myself that if their friend only knew that they have become the subject of a 'focus group' of sorts, they would feel a sick betrayal.

People are not projects. If you knew that, no matter what, your 'friend' would never become a Christian would you still be their friend? It's no different than a group of adolescent boys engaged in locker room talk bragging about how close they are to adding their current 'girlfriend' to their collection of belt notches.

In too many ways the church has become an exclusive sub-culture that is appearance based. You will know they are Christians by what they do and don't do, where they go and don't go, who they associate with and who they disassociate. Whatever happened to letting them know you're a Christian 'by [your] love, by [your] love'? To the rest of the world, they have the disturbing appearance of being a group of one-dimensional robots where actions don't line up with words. Usually it's too much for any average outsider to stomach and that's why you hear them talk about the church being full of hypocrites.

It kills me when I hear that, mostly because they're right. What neither group understands is that God isn't looking at what you're doing wrong, He is taking inventory of the intentions in your heart. The members of the church know that the public is scrutinizing them, so they come up with a strict set of rules, a moral code to live by. Every church denomination has one and they're all different.

The list of things that are discouraged range from not going to a movie theater to not drinking caffeinated beverages. They're designed to administer some sort of control on self and others. What happens, then, is that authentic relationship with God becomes unnecessary when all you have to do is follow the formula, appear like everyone else and fly under the radar. If a person learns the language and sticks to the dress code and rules of conductivity then they don't really need to know Jesus. When a member of this sub-culture fails, especially publicly, then they are mercilessly shunned.

They are at each other's throats about the most irrelevant things and they never get to the real focus. The unbeliever is criticizing the believer for not being blameless and the believer is trying to find ways to escape the criticism.

I can't tell you how many times I've heard it said to the younger generations of believers that the best way to be a witness of your faith is to carry your Bible or wear a witnessing t-shirt. It's the appearance of claiming a side.

I understand the mentality. It's about knowing that you're on a 'battle ground' and you are waving the flag of your home country letting anyone who sees you know that you are a 'warrior' ready to throw down for Jesus in a trendy, 'extreme' kind of way. It's an exciting war cry heard throughout church camps and conventions all over. It's easy to just go with that religious excitement and stomp your feet on an imaginary devil head to a catchy, well lead song. What I'm wondering is who do you think you're fighting, or scaring for that matter, by your flags and shirts and feet stomping? Satan doesn't care what you wear or what you carry when your appearance and behavior alone are enough to keep the outsiders freaked out and alienated enough to maintain their distance.

Who is going to be the salt of the earth? Who is going to be a presence in the 'world' and be a voice that is actually heard? This problem with appearances runs so deep it makes me wonder if there is any bigger obstacle in front of the believer. What nobody is thinking is that the only being you have to please is the one who has the power over your eternal life. It's an endless cycle of the church being attacked and the outsider feeling lied to. What a dirty way to keep both of them busy on the unimportant aspects of life and the real truths go unexplored and real freedom goes unlived.

chapter fifteen
role playing

"All we're saying is that God has the first word, initiating the action
in which we play our part for good or ill." – Romans 9:18

The truth about God has been right in front of us the whole time, yet we are literally incapable of grasping who He actually is. It's like trying to fit a NASA navigation program into a Commodore 64. Our minds do not have the memory or speed to keep up with that much information. We are reduced to hunting and pecking at bits of truth and making pathetic attempts to fit them into some sort of coherent belief system. It's fine as long as you know that's what is happening.

If you do your best to find and teach Godly truth knowing that you've only got it partially right and admitting that the system you've set up is flawed then you keep yourself and the people you influence open to learning more. It is a life of trial and error, of falling down and getting back up. It is one of the biggest challenges for a believer, who feels he has 'arrived' to see the Truth when it is right in front of him. Maintaining a commendable level of successful Christian living is the exact place where he stops growing.

I am confident in the information I'm putting in these chapters, however, I have to acknowledge that I have blind spots even if I'm not aware of them. My life experience and my spiritual vision are impairing my ability to see the truth in its perfection. I'm doing my best to keep my words grounded in scripture, but if I'm to believe that same scripture, I have no choice but to admit there must be things about which I am not one hundred percent correct. James chapter three says, "We get it wrong nearly every time we open our mouths. If you could find someone whose speech was perfectly true, you'd have a perfect person, in perfect control of life." The upside to getting it wrong is when you get to learn something new when you go about correcting it.

∽─❦❧❦─∾

It's hard to imagine anything more important than worship in a believer's life. You can sing that God is worthy of your praise but can you come to terms with the fact that you are not even worthy to carry His shoes? Would you try to defend that right? What would you bring in your defense to support your case? If all of your good deeds, sacrifices and honorable mentions aren't what He wants, then what do you have to offer? The answer is 'nothing.' The 'Great Reversal' is at work again.

There is a praise and worship song that describes God as 'all powerful' and 'untamable.' Is He untamable as long as He stays predictable? Is He all-powerful except when others sin and then that sin has the ungodly authority to re-route things? This suggests that God's ultimate desire, an original plan, is contingent upon man's obedience. If the King of Kings and Lord of Lords detailed an orderly method for achieving His overall objective, do you think that capricious man has the power to trump it?

It's absurd to think you can change God's course.

Is it possible that God uses sin to carry out his purpose? In the first chapter of Acts, Peter is about to replace Judas. He is in a room with about a hundred and twenty others and when he mentions Judas he starts off by reminding them of when David wrote about the one who would guide the men who arrested Jesus. It wasn't a surprise to God when Judas betrayed Jesus. It wasn't a surprise to Jesus, either. He knew the scriptures and the order in which things would happen and this was part of it. Peter is speaking to the people in the room and says, "That scripture had to be fulfilled, and now has been. Judas was one of us and had his assigned place in this ministry."

We know that God has a plan, He sets the scene and lays out the terrain and we follow along walking exactly where He knows we'll walk and choosing exactly what He knows we'll choose. We are experiencing in real time what God has already seen in eternity. We don't know what lies ahead, but He does. In his book, Rumors of Another World, Philip Yancey wrote about a jog he took through some fields of a sheep farm in Australia.

> "As I jogged, it occurred to me that sheep, to the degree they think at all, may well presume they order their own destiny. They chew cud, roam the fields, make choices, and live out their lot with only a few rude interruptions from dogs, devils, rams, and humans. Little do they know that the entire scenario, from birth to death and every stage in between, is being orchestrated according to a rational plan by the humans who live in the ranch house.
>
> C.S. Lewis conjectured, 'There may be Natures piled upon Natures, each supernatural to the one beneath it.' Do we stand in relation to God as sheep

stand in relation to us? The Bible suggests that in some ways we do. 'It is [God] who made us, and we are his; we are his people, the sheep of his pasture,' Note the possessives: his people, his pasture. According to this point of view, we live out our days in a world owned by another. We may insist on autonomy- 'we all like sheep have gone astray' –but in the end that autonomy is no more impressive, or effective, than the autonomy of a Tasmanian ewe.

If God exists, and if our planet represents God's work of art, we will never grasp why we are here without taking that reality into account."

The idea that God is in control is more embraceable when you think of it in the context of future blessings or situations that have a positive effect on you. It's harder to accept the truth of God's sovereignty when you're going through your own personal hell. However, the truth doesn't change based on your perspective. He knows exactly what is going on and how to turn it to benefit you in the long run.

How big of a risk taker do you think God can be in His dealings with the lives of people? Have you ever wondered if God strategically places people in different spots and uses their failures to ensure that His purpose is achieved? Have you ever been slowed down or pushed off course only to find that you missed a horrific tragedy by the exact time that you were detained and found what you were looking for when you veered off track? Do you think these things are all coincidence?

Your purse disappears and you spend at least twenty minutes searching for it before you determine that it must have been stolen. You feel vulnerable and creepy thinking that someone was able to get that close to what you thought was safe and takes it from you. Luckily your keys weren't in your purse and you're able to take your three year old to her little dance class. As you're on your way you pass a terrible car accident. It appears that a truck was going through the intersection, exactly where you are traveling and got t-boned by an SUV that ran a red light.

You feel the hair stand up on the back of your neck as you realize that if you had not been searching for your stolen purse, it would have been you who got hit. Only in that accident, there's no way that your little car could have stood up to the SUV quite like the truck did. You glance in your rearview mirror and block the 'what if's' from your imagination as you look at your little girls tiny face. For the moment you're aware that Someone must be looking out for you.

What about the guy who stole your purse? Is he a bad guy? Absolutely. He stole your purse. But, what about that timing? Did God use the sin of a purse thief to save your life? Would He do that? That causes so many questions because you have to wonder if God made the thief steal or if He knew he would steal and didn't protect you from it.

God doesn't 'make' people do anything. He knows what you'll do in any given situation. Why wouldn't God protect you from a low-life blatant thief? Well, I'm suggesting that God uses sin for His purposes. This is an example of God working out all things for the good of those who love Him and taking what was meant for evil and using it for your good. (Romans 8:28, Genesis 50:20)

I wonder if God used Judas to play the bad guy in the scriptures. Scripture had to be fulfilled. The plan had to be carried out. God knows who will be with Him in the end and who will not. Would God, with His final knowledge of Judas, use him to do what he did? Proverbs 21:18 (NIV) says, "The wicked become a ransom for the righteous, and the unfaithful for the upright." In Isaiah 43 God is speaking to the Israelites telling them how much He loves them. He says in verses three and four, "I give Egypt for your ransom... Since you are precious and honored in my sight, and because I love you, I will give men in exchange for you, and people in exchange for your life."

You can't say that something is outside of God's will because all we know about God's will is that He wants to unite his creation with him. Do you not think He will use whatever means necessary to make that happen? If you were lost in the dark in the middle of nowhere with your enemy hunting you down, intent on destroying you, would you want your rescuer to play nice and not step on toes while He skips along eating Skittles or would you want Him to move Heaven and Earth to find you and bring you home?

God moves Heaven and Earth for us, it's not always pretty, but who are you to question His methods? He knows what He needs to do and we don't, so we have to trust Him.

♁ ❦❦❦ ♁

We think we have things figured out and we walk along making god decisions and god judgments and congratulating our god selves on the way we are pleasing God all the while living a thoughtless, unintelligent, one-dimensional faith that excludes anyone who has a stream of shortcomings.

When you consciously make a decision to stop trying to become what you want to be or think you should be and you open your mind to the infiniteness of God's complete control then He will empty you of yourself and fill you up with Him. You cannot do that on your own. The only way that you can see your undeniable and inconsolable need for Jesus is to see who you really are without Him.

Make no mistake; coming face to face with that actuality is excruciating. You can't experience God's immeasurable grace without being crushed under the pressure of your own sin. Saying that you are unclean doesn't make it a part of your reality unless you can look inside yourself and confess where you are nefarious. This confession isn't to be confused with the ramblings of someone mindlessly reciting the churchy propaganda that is drained of sincerity and bled of any real influence.

If you have firsthand knowledge of your need for and God given right to the free gift of grace and its life saving, life giving power your message is going to be laced with authentic and recognizable emotion that someone will find familiar and will connect to. Your personal experience with the power of Jesus and His grace will catch on and spread. It will aid in uniting people under one truth, that truth being that God sent his son Jesus to pay the price for your sins long before you committed them. It is one price paid for all and the only way to have eternal life is to believe in that truth.

You can have a limited understanding of that truth and have an equally relative response, but your speech will not sound like everybody else's. It's hard to explain what has happened inside of you when you become a believer because what has happened is bigger than you are and bigger than your vocabulary. It's actually entertaining to hear a new Christian try to come up with analogies for the indescribable difference they see and feel in their lives.

However, my stomach sinks when I hear a new believer start to talk like everybody else they've heard in the church. They may even plump their speech with buttery extremes regarding their previous sinful condition. They summons a few tears to aid in dramatic effect when telling their 'coming to Jesus' story and repeat a few snazzy phrases they've heard about this sort of thing. I understand how it works because I've witnessed it many times over and have even played my own role in the charade.

If I were to analyze the mentality behind the church role-playing problem I would think that the new believer feels a bit lacking and wants to appear that she has arrived to the place where everybody else is. She begins imitating the others around her and joins them as they perform their way into the religious clique. That's when I know that they're either on an emotional ride that they will eventually fall from or they have been sucked into the mindless and heartless culture and they'll soon begin collecting badges for their good deeds vest.

The problems come when one of them decides to be real. When they start to wiggle out of the probing church hands and crack off some of the alter call crust. Real questions about real situations and real failures have no place in the snicker doodle mothball world they've trapped themselves in. What if someone asked you why you liked them more after they faked 'falling down in the spirit'? The question would be turned on them, like they had the problem. Well, you're right, they shouldn't have faked it. Now, answer the question.

If someone has real questions and the trinket answer you gave them doesn't hush them, then there must be something wrong with their relationship with Jesus, right? You shiver at the thought you almost had and thank God that you don't have such deep piercing questions in your non-analytical mind.

A person that has a real desire to know God and search His depths will have the opportunity to do so. You don't have to be afraid of asking real questions. A lot of times I see the church protecting their theology from piercing minds by making you feel inferior for having the questions in the first place.

It's important to me that you know that God can withstand your beautifully piercing mind. He can withstand it because not only does He have the answers, He set up a whole world of riddles and clues for you to follow on your discovery expedition toward knowing Him. All of creation has been set as a discovery paradise from science and medicine to art and music. You see, He has a beautifully piercing mind, too.

Choose a direction and walk in it. Shake every mystery out of every dusty corner and ask questions. Ask things that challenge your beliefs and could have potentially deadly answers. No one should be afraid of a quizzical mind unless you're afraid that what you want them to believe isn't real.

If a person can abandon everything they lay claim to, including the faith system they've carefully designed, to search for the truth, no matter what that truth may be, I guarantee it will be the most exhilarating experience of their lives. Abandon your preconceived ideas and jump off the cliff of safety. If you want something real, you will find it.

✢

Jonah was a prophet whom God told to deliver a warning to a city that was engaged in evil. God wanted him to go and warn them that He was going to destroy them if they didn't turn from the evil that occupied them. Jonah knew that God would save them if they responded to the warning and he didn't think they deserved it. Jonah ignored God and got on a boat traveling in the opposite direction. When God surrounded the boat with a storm the men panicked. They threw things overboard and prayed to their own god's.

When they learned that Jonah served the God who made the land and the sea, he volunteered to be thrown over in order to save the others. They hesitated and tried to row the boat back to shore. When that didn't work they reluctantly threw Jonah into the sea telling Jonah's God that he was in His hands. As soon as his body hit the water the sea calmed completely. The men on the boat were in such awe of Jonah's God that they began to worship Him making sacrifices and vows.

Jonah, in the belly of the fish, cried out in passion and love to the God whose love and grace saved him. He told God that he'd do what was asked of him and deliver the message to the city. Jonah, until that point, wasn't in touch with what it was like to need to be rescued by God.

His newly discovered need salted his message. It was a message that was now a lot more powerful than if he reluctantly went when he was told. Jonah's run in with grace made his words more effective. Jonah was a grace hoarder because he didn't see a need for it in his own life. Those in need of grace give it freely.

When he ran, was Jonah on the verge of messing up God's plan for the Ninevites or was God sovereignly using Jonah's failure to transform him into who he needed to be for the job He sent him to do? I guess it comes down to the whether or not you believe in coincidence. Is this stuff an accident worked out in a nice way, or was someone's failure used to display God's glory? Is this God scrambling to make your little mistake into something happy or is it all part of the process?

Some believe that God goes behind you and cleans up your messes. Others believe that He goes before you and sets things up for you. God is omnipresent. Therefore, by definition, He does both.

Matthew chapter five says that believers are designed to be salt seasoning that bring out the God flavors of the earth. If you limit your knowledge of God to the feel good, sunshine moments then you are missing half of the story. He's not a dancing monkey out trying to get everybody to feel good and fall in love under rainbows. He's not limited to being the Lamb of God because He's also the Lion of Judah. His concern is to bring you to a place where you know Him. You must be emptied of yourself and filled up with Him. Don't underestimate the process in which you are emptied of yourself. They don't call it death for dramatic flair.

When you decided to give your heart to Jesus and you said a sweet prayer of surrender and told God that He could do whatever He wanted in your life. You may have sang a little song and offered up your gifts and goodness to Him telling Him to send you out into the world. I've had that moment of surrender myself.

I remember a time when I was conscious of God speaking to me and asking me if there were conditions on that surrender. He wanted to know if He could do it on His terms. In essence, do I really give up my right to my life and who I am to be whatever He needs me to be? And do I realize that it means that He gets to pick the terms? I thought I did understand. I know now that I didn't, but I wouldn't take it back.

I was driving down the street several months ago. I was in the rebuilding stages of the aftermath of my fall and I wondered where God was in all of this mess. It is one thing to know that you've been forgiven and that you do still have a future, but it's another to be in the middle of the mess with absolutely no clue how God is going to clean it up. What I've learned about God is that He never said He'd make it easy on us. If He has a reason for us to suffer, then we're going to suffer.

I was crying and praying while I drove circles around my neighborhood. My prayer used the same words as it did before, but this time the meaning, passion and tone were different. I kept saying, 'Oh, my gosh, God, you really *can* do whatever you want with my life.' It was a prayer of trembling and realization. It wasn't me giving permission to God; it was me becoming aware of His authority over me.

What if He's fashioned me to be in constant difficulty because that's how I'm the most useful to Him? Do I still surrender or do I bail? I can't refute the fact that He is God therefore I can't not surrender. This is where trust comes in. This is the spot where I can worship God as He is molding and carving me into someone that He can use.

We're not in relationship with a God who sticks to formulas or rules and He is most definitely not conventional. He is intensely unfathomable and we're just us, but for some reason He delights in us.

There are plenty of times when you might see your circumstances and wonder how someone could love you and let you suffer so much. If you only look at what you can see and touch, then you're missing the whole thing. The enemy operates on that level of your perception. He knows the ins and outs of every aspect of what is in the physical world. There is another existence that we can't see or touch, yet we are playing roles in it right now.

If this world dies and the spiritual realm does not, then it's in the spiritual realm that is real and the one we can touch is a distraction. Can you see how your strength here and now is a huge handicap in the spirit world? You fight against things that you see and feel here without having a clue of what they look like on the other side.

Jesus says the same thing in John chapter 8, "You decide according to what you see and touch. I don't make judgments like that...I wouldn't make judgments out of the narrowness of my experience but in the largeness of the One who sent me, the Father." He says it again a bit later, "You live on terms of what you see and touch... you're missing God in your lives."

Things here on earth are not like they are in the spirit. They are beyond backward. Maybe that's why God has to physically or emotionally break you in the flesh before you are of any use to Him in the spirit.

If you're scared of His power and control, which you should be, then remember you can trust Him. You have a choice when it comes to your focus. You can study your situation, your ability to measure up to the huge abyss between what you can do and what needs to be done, or you can look at God. No expectations, no promise of rewards for being a do-gooder, no bonus for going the extra mile. When you're flying through the air and are about to crash on the rocks, is He still God or do you want your life back? That's the real question.

I'm not the first or the last person to use this example, but I love it and it's a perfect fit. C.S. Lewis wrote in his book, 'The Lion the Witch and the Wardrobe', a part where the beaver family was telling the children about the Lion, Aslan. They wanted to know how they should approach him and they asked if he was safe. Mr. Beaver responded by saying, "Who said anything about being safe? 'Course he isn't *safe*. But he's *good*." You can't control God. He is not a tame 'lion'. But you can trust Him because He is good.

God knows exactly what needs to be done in order to transform you into something He can use. We all have been created with a purpose but we are not born with the ability to carry it out. Your job is to continually let go of yourself. A great way to keep from getting in the way is to try to recognize Him in everything. We are in a process that never reaches completeness while we are alive.

We are all in different places at different times. Sometimes we can say that we are innocent and other times we can see where we're the ones who do wrong. The danger with seeing yourself as the victim is becoming self righteous and vengeful when trying to preserve your life as you know it. When someone sins against you, it's better for you to keep yourself open for more abuse.

I know that doesn't make sense but, the power to do that comes from knowing that God can take care of you better than you can you can take care of yourself. You have to trust Him to do that. It's a way to submit yourself to Him exactly like He asks.

One common misconception that believers have is that God wouldn't allow one of His beloved children to be beat up by some sinner, or wouldn't let any evil motives near you. So, when you do fall prey to another's sin you fail to see God's hand molding you, therefore rejecting every aspect of the hardship that was dished out to you. Your response to another's sin against you has the potential to prolong the effects of the sin.

Go ahead and hate the sin but, do not equate the sin with the sinner. The sinner needs you to do the impossible and display the mercy, grace and love of God in order to conquer the evil. If you do not take every inhuman action to diminish the effects of the sin, then you carry out the evil that was intended by the Evil One. When God comes in to right the wrongs, He'll have to 'right' you, too. When God sets you straight it hurts far worse than the pain from the sin against you. Reach out and love the unlovable, it's the only way you can stay blameless.

This is your opportunity to 'rejoice' when others sin against you. You can identify with Jesus who went through unbelievable suffering. Jesus is no stranger to being the recipient of the deadly blow that sin delivers. This is your opportunity to play Jesus and choke out a prayer that says, 'Forgive them, Father.' Welcome the sinner back and use the opportunity to show them how Jesus would treat them. The Bible says that good conquers evil. Put it to the test and worship while you watch divine love erase sin.

There is another misconception that, if you truly are a purely devoted follower of Christ, you will not be overcome by evil and carry out sin. So, when you find yourself in that situation there is a tendency to feel so much shame that you want to give up. There are so many questions that arise and you ultimately question where God was and what your sin says about you.

My message to the sinner is simply this: You can believe Jesus when He says that He will forgive you over and over and over and over. There is nothing you can do that would make Him walk away from you. Others will and they'll tell you that you couldn't possibly be sorry enough. That is a direct contradiction to the life, death and resurrection of Jesus and no matter who claims to be speaking for Him it is absolutely false and he is a fraud.

Don't let your faith fail and, when you come back, use the lessons you have learned to strengthen others. Whether your life is being shifted by another's sin or your own sin has brought you to a place of discovering God, there is hope because you are becoming someone that you could have never become otherwise. You have to wait until it happens. Mine happened when I took a huge public stumble. It was the most backward thing I've ever experienced by it happening that way, but my life got real when I fell.

I know my place, without question, and it's certainly not in a place of high esteem or honor. I almost laugh at the thought of those words being applied to me. I do know that God permeates more of my existence than He ever has and I know who I am to Him and that's enough for me. Who I am to Him is not who I see in the mirror. I'm lost to the old girl. I'm no longer sad about that and I won't go searching for her to rebuild her reputation. I've died to my flesh, just like He asked.

chapter sixteen
when loss is gain

"...whoever wants to save his life will lose it, but whoever loses his life for me will find it." - Matthew 16:25

Everything we do wrong is sin, but not all sin is fatal. (1 John 5:17) The only requirement to be in good standing with God is to believe that Jesus is His son. Jesus cancels a believer's sin and God's doesn't consider it. The most difficult thing about this truth is that it's hard for us, in our human condition, to believe that God isn't keeping score. The sin itself has no power, but our response to it is what carries the most potential for damage.

Sin is a slave to grace. The aftermath of sin is like a horror flick. You can let yourself go for the ride or you can shut it off. We have a spiritual enemy that has one purpose and that purpose is to destroy you.

You will sin. It's a fact. You do, you are and you will and anyone who disputes that is deceived. If you understand that your belief in Jesus puts you in a place where your sin is cancelled out, then your enemy, Satan, has no power over you. If you think that you damage your relationship with Jesus with your sin, then you are a prime target for Satan to come in and tell you that you're ruined.

If you could damage your relationship with Jesus with sin, then why was He crucified? Did He die so that you could continue your rule-keeping, peer pleasing religion?

> *"Is it not clear to you that to go back to that old rule-keeping, peer-pleasing religion would be an abandonment of everything personal and free in my relationship with God? I refuse to do that, to repudiate God's grace. If a living relationship with God could come by rule-keeping, then Christ died unnecessarily."*
> *- Galatians 2:21*

Jesus didn't give His life for the upright. They don't need Him, not to mention that they don't exist. Jesus died for the ones that those who consider themselves 'upright' won't associate with.

If you take a plain white sheet of paper and make a map of the places in your life where you are a moral failure and then take a red marker and blot out the 'cities' of sin on your map, how much of your paper would be red? The red represents the lifeblood of Jesus, therefore the more failure you have in your life the more area Jesus covers. If you lined up a group of people with varied life maps and had them hold it high, who do you think would feel like they could stand tall in the presence of God? Obviously the people who are a living moral success would be pretty proud of their efforts. However, God is looking for the red, not the
right. The least of men become the greatest, the greatest become the least.

There is such a thing as fatal sin. Fatal sin is when a person who does not believe in Jesus sins. Theirs is a lifestyle of sin. It's a lifestyle of sin because Jesus is not in the lives of those who don't believe in Him. If you are a believer and you sin, then your sin is not fatal. A believer does not make sin a lifestyle.

∽─❀❧❀─∾

When I went outside of my marriage and had an affair, I came to a point where I could not go on. I didn't know what to do about my feelings or the damage I caused, but I did know I could not continue in my sin. I am a woman who is obviously capable of taking a wrong turn, but, because of my relationship with Jesus, I could not continue down that road. I would have to sever my relationship with Him in order to go any further.

During my affair I would not talk to God. In my heart I knew I was hiding. I was like Eve, crouched in shame behind a bush. Then, I heard God call out my name, as though the grass under my feet and the leaves in my hair hadn't told their creator where His little girl was hiding. I couldn't continue to sin because my Father came searching for me. If I didn't have a relationship with Him, then I wouldn't know what His voice sounded like and I wouldn't respond when I heard it. He called my name and I came out from my hiding spot.

Satan whispered his sexy song of seduction and lured me into the dark with promises of a safe return. I listened to the breath in my ear as it tickled my neck and weakened my knees and I heard what I wanted to hear.

He told me that there was nowhere I could go that would be too far. He told me to not be afraid because, if I fell, I could get back up. His words were true but the God proclaimed 'Father of Lies' left out one important bit of information. He never told me about the legions of forces that would be holding me down once I fell. I never knew that the strength of my own 'goodness' would be wrapped around my neck. I saw no hint of the condemnation that would come from ninety-nine percent of the people I loved. 'Oh, from the heights you've fallen,' they'd say, 'what hell to have to live with what you've done.'

And where was my seducer now? Where was the tantalizing voice that was supposed to stick up for me? In the light of day I could see him smirking behind the crowd as he turned on his heel and headed for the door. I realized who he was and the words 'Another One Bites the Dust' on the back of his t-shirt mocked me as I watched him walked away.

There were no words of reasoning I could use to bargain with. I could not justify my actions. What was done was done. I stood out in the open while curls of smoke drifted up from the pistol on my hip and juice from the forbidden fruit drew flies to my lips. What does a person do when there is no justification for their actions?

Accepting grace is getting off too easy. It's not like I stole a candy bar. It doesn't mean much when people tell me that all sins are equal. Those are the people who didn't get hurt by it. Just think about having a conversation with my ex-husband and asking him if he would rather I got caught stealing from a store or sleeping with another man.

Sins aren't supposed to have weight, but in the lives of friends and lovers, they most certainly do and saying the contrary is as contrived as a condescending would-be who gets a buzz off of being a little bit better than everybody else.

❧

This afternoon I watched a movie I've already

seen. The first time I watched it was before my fall. It's about a woman who moved with her daughter from Mexico to Los Angeles and ends up working as a housekeeper for a family. In the story, the woman doesn't speak English and that keeps her detached from the family for most of the movie.

The husband and wife have no connection, the wife and her daughter have a strained relationship and, to sum their family, up, they are just about normal. When I watched it for the first time I loved it because it was real. It dealt with the honest emotions one has as a woman, a wife and a mother.

As the movie unfolds, the main character and the man in the family she works for realize that they have fallen in love. They acknowledge their feelings one evening and make comments about how the other sees things in them that they always wished could be seen.

In a world where you can do things for yourself and search for your own happiness, they would be understood if they were to make the decision to be together. However, as I said, the movie was real and the main character made a hard decision before they crossed the point of no return. She made a comment about how she no longer lived for herself, she was a mother and that meant she had to walk away.

She quit her job, said her good-byes and as she was walking down the street, she could walk tall. She was a good woman and even though the decision she made was hard, she did the right thing and could lie down, wake up and look at herself in the mirror with no regret.

I did not walk away like the woman in the movie. Unlike her, I could not go to bed without my obese grief lying down on top me. I could not get up without my mourning greeting me with a steel-toe boot to the stomach. There was a time when I knew exactly who I was and

I liked me. I could no longer stand to be in my own skin. I could not look in my mirror and see any fleck of resemblance to the woman I once was. It was as though I died and I had to let go.

The thing that makes the least amount of sense is how I could think that the things I thought were worthy of someone's love were the things I had to trade away to get it. I was a good wife and a good mother. I knew I was attractive and desirable. However, I was in a marriage where I felt invisible. My husband wasn't interested in who I actually was, he just liked the package I provided.

One of the biggest things that made me vulnerable to an affair was that the outsider saw all of those things. I felt someone fall in love with the real me. The twist came when I crossed that line and ceased to be a good wife and a good mom. Where is the pride and honor in that? The exact qualities I thought worthy of being seen disappeared when I showed them.

The biggest battle I faced during the aftermath was having the strength to believe the simplicity of Jesus' story of redemption. I had a lot of opposition. My own self-judgment was one of my worst enemies. I believed that I would never do such a thing as I did. I thought I was better than that. I thought my faith was stronger than that. I trusted myself and I felt like my own body was disloyal to me. The other people whose trust I betrayed were able to find consolation by cutting off the painful wound I became, but I could not escape myself.

I found that my heart would not stop beating for me and my lungs would not rest. When I would go to the Bible to find some direction, I found grace. Grace became a word that stirred up anger in me. My friends, the only believers or Christians that I knew, turned the message of grace into a lie. Everything that the Bible says about people like me, sinners, was defied by every person I knew who claimed to be a Christian. I discovered what 'don't let your faith fail' meant. It meant 'believe Me, not them.'

⚜

When I was seventeen and living with my friend and her abusive boyfriend, I watched him drag her across the floor by her hair and choke the breath out of her neck with his hands. Sitting in the same room was his friend. I couldn't overpower a man in a fit of rage because I'm too small, but the other grown man could and he didn't. I have the same sick feeling about the one who sat on his hands as the one who beat with his hands. Even if you're not the one spreading the word of another's failure and you're not sending her messages of dismissal, you're still lumped in the same category because you are standing there and letting it happen.

Out of the thousands of people Justin knew through his job in a Christian rock band, two people sought him out and gave him a message. Justin knows countless people across the United States who used to vie for his attention. He knew hundreds of church organizations and leaders on a personal level.

Out of all of the church 'company men' that he knew, not a single one uttered a word to him. Not a message of unmerited grace to be heard. As a matter of fact, they are an awkward presence or they pretend to not know him. The only people who found their way to get a message to him were (at the time) a guy who sells truck accessories and a photographer. I'll use the words of the former to illustrate what I believe that Jesus would have said, "Justin, I hate what you've done but I love you. And you will always have a friend in me."

"Go after those who take the wrong way. Be tender with sinners, but not soft on sin," (Jude 1:23).

I don't blame people for not knowing what to say to us. I wouldn't either. At least they weren't like Mitch whose words spit burning acid on wounded spirits. Galatians 4:17 warns about people like that, "They want to shut you out of the free world of God's grace so that you will always depend on them for approval and direction, making them feel important." The best thing you can do for someone when they fall is be patient. Don't give up on them. The only person that would hold someone down when they fell is someone who has something to gain from their failure.

⌒─❦❧─⌒

I've shared my story with a small number of people over the past couple of years and something that people always want to know is how in the world my faith didn't fail through all of this. A broad way to answer that is my relationship is with Jesus not Jesus through a church. My relationship with Him is real and it's clearest when I'm all alone. If I didn't have something real and internal to base things on, then I would have rejected anything God related with a violent slam of the door to my life. In my world, the church can be (and is) riddled with flaws but it doesn't shake my faith in God. It certainly did and does shake my faith in the people, however, and anything that resembles 'churchiness' triggers my gag reflex. I find it sparkling on the outside and hollow and dusty on the inside.

The only reason I have a church home is because a pastor came up to Justin one day. He knew what Justin had done and wanted him to know that he knew it would be difficult for him to find a church that would accept him. He told him that he would always be welcome at his church. They now have a talented drummer and sound guy on their worship team rotation.

The more direct answer for why my faith didn't fail through my experience is because Jesus, in the verse He gave me in October 1996 told me that He was praying it wouldn't. Through that message I learned that God knew what I would do. He knew that the spiritual battle would rage around me; and Diane's 'flashing yellow light' vision told me that Jesus knew that He could lose me in that intersection. I had to deny the words of my old friends and the voice of my own understanding to not let my faith fail. Through the truth that I've learned since my fall I know now that Jesus had a purpose in all of this and that gave me the strength to make it through.

I spent a lot of nights crying and asking God to put things back to the way they were. If I hadn't been pregnant, if my ex-husband would have left school to come fight for me, if I had more money, I would have moved Heaven and Earth to set things according to what I and many others thought 'right' would be. I would have backtracked to my old life and tried to pick up where it left off. I may never know God's purposes in everything, but I do know that He did not want me to walk backward, He wanted me to walk forward and He determined my steps for me.

This entire experience has recreated me. I'm still learning who this new woman is and I find my answers as the Bible sheds light on them. What I have experienced is the place where death becomes life. When guilt or accusation resurface in the form of my own thoughts or in the faces or words of the people who once knew me I can remind myself that my sin has no power over me because Jesus took it. It is dead and what is dead cannot define me.

I've been given a gift through this. I have a freedom that comes from letting go of every bit of who I was and living in the truth of what God has revealed. What's even more amazing about this is that I cannot, for a second, get any bit of pride from it because of how it came to me. "Satan's angel did his best to get me down; what he in fact did was push me to my knees." (2 Corinthians 12:7) I gave in to my death and grabbed hold of the life that Jesus offers. I found God through losing my hold on my sense of self.

I can't explain reasons for everything that has happened in my life. I'm confident that I know very little. I've learned the meaning of humility. If Jesus were still walking the earth and asked me to join Him for a stroll it would take more pride for me to say no than it would to be seen in public with him. Not because of Him, however, but because of my fear of what people would think of me. They would whisper among themselves, 'Who does she think she is?'

I wonder if this is how Zacchaeus felt when Jesus singled him out to for a lunch date. Or maybe this is how the sinful woman in Luke chapter seven felt when the Pharisees whispered about her as she anointed the feet of Jesus. The religious people accused Jesus many times of being a 'friend of sinners'. I had a hard time going to church because of the way it felt to have everyone know what I did. When I would pray about it I felt the voice of God speak in to me and say that He wouldn't leave my side and if they glare at me or whisper about me they're doing it to Him, too. He let me know that He'd take what I get and I wouldn't be alone. When they looked at me, they saw me standing by myself, but I knew who was standing next to me and that made them not matter anymore.

The story of the prodigal son in Luke chapter fifteen came to life for me when I was trying to understand why the church rejects people who do something wrong.

The part of the story that I hadn't heard before was where the brother refuses to join the party celebrating the prodigal's return. Jesus told this story as an analogy of what it's like for other people when a believer wanders off and then tries to come back.

> *"The older brother became angry and refused to go in. So his father went out and pleaded with him. But he answered his father, 'Look! All these years I've been slaving for you and never disobeyed your orders. Yet you never gave me even a young goat so I could celebrate with my friends. But when this son of yours who has squandered your property with prostitutes comes home, you kill the fattened calf for him!' 'My son,' the father said, 'you are always with me, and everything I have is yours. But we had to celebrate and be glad, because this brother of yours was dead and is alive again; he was lost and is found.'"(Luke 15:28-32)*

If you want to be like Jesus, then read about Him. Find out for yourself what the truth is and learn how to sift through the religious fluff and fillers. I've heard people say over and over that they are afraid that, by being a friend to Justin or me, they would get judged for appearing like they are 'condoning' our sin. They are worried about their public appearance. It's true that they would get talked about for being a friend of sinners, just like Jesus was.

Diane admits to not knowing what 'forgiveness looks like in this situation.' Forgiveness in the Bible 'looks like' restoration and says "if you're too good for that, you are badly deceived." (Galatians 6:1) Romans 5:20 calls grace 'aggressive forgiveness.' "Master, how many times do I forgive a brother or sister who hurts me? Seven?" Jesus replied, "Seven! Hardly. Try seventy times seven."

(Matthew 18:21-22) "If a fellow believer hurts you, go and tell him—work it out between the two of you. If he listens, you've made a friend. If he won't listen, take one or two others along so that the presence of witnesses will keep things honest, and try again. If he still won't listen, tell the church. If he won't listen to the church, you'll have to start over from scratch, confront him with the need for repentance, and offer again God's forgiving love." (Matthew 18:15-17)

I don't doubt Diane's struggle. Mitch is her brother. Mitch is married to Anne. Diane has a remarkable amount of loyalty to her family. She wants to do the 'godly' thing but is finding it difficult to know how to take action and juggle her loyalties. Here's a thought, if you can't be godly in a specific situation, then maybe you are in an ungodly situation.

The 'Great Reversal' is at work again. "Anyone who sacrifices... *family*... because of me will get it all back a hundred times over, not to mention the considerable bonus of eternal life." (Matthew 19:29, emphasis mine)

chapter seventeen
crime and punishment

If we give up and turn our backs on all we've learned, all we've been given, all the truth we now know, we repudiate Christ's sacrifice and are left on our own to face the Judgment. – Hebrews 10:26

I heard a guy preaching on the radio a few months ago and he was talking about being sick of people saying that Christians aren't supposed to judge one another. He said that we have spiritual insight for a reason and we can discern whether someone is right with God and when they're not. He tried to back his ideas up with scripture, but he used half of a sentence from the New Testament and an out of context half quote from Moses in the Old Testament.

He spoke with authority and in a way that would make you feel stupid if you didn't see it his way. In the background I heard the group he was preaching to audibly agreeing with him. I pictured those people going to work the next morning equipped with the authorizing instructions to start categorizing people according to their perception.

The other morning I was sipping coffee and watching T.V. on my couch. A preacher stared into the camera and said that he believed that 'the key to prosperity, deliverance from depression and all sorts of mental illnesses, a happy marriage, and physical health' were all found in Romans. I have a friend who was told that her miscarriage was evidence of sin in her life. Another woman asked her church to pray that she and her husband would be able to conceive but was told that all she needed to do was 'get in the river.' These same people can preach warnings about false prophets and never realize that that's exactly what they are.

It's amazing how a preacher can preach for an hour and say nothing. When he does say something that is right on point, it's surrounded by sentences that water it down and cancel it out. I heard a message not too long ago where the preacher told his audience that everything happens in God's time. He could have explained that fact by describing God's sovereignty but he didn't. I was anticipating that he would then remind them of who God is, thereby easing the concern for their personal well being and shifting all of that energy into focusing on God. His next sentence cancelled out his first. He explained that everything happens in God's time because people have the freedom to choose. He cancelled out God's authority by saying that things are determined by the choices of men.

I understand that we have the freedom to make our own choices, but have you ever considered who is determining what you are choosing between?

I've heard people try to explain what the Bible means regarding freedom by saying that when you live according to a set of rules your freedom comes from not having to endure the pain of failure from breaking the rules. They say that a relationship with God keeps you from sinning and therefore you experience freedom from sin. Have we created a religion that doesn't need Jesus? That's not freedom, that's self-control. Jesus wasn't the atonement in case you accidently sin. He was the atonement because you hopelessly sin. The freedom that the Bible is talking about is not something you earn by making the right choices; the freedom is the lack of punishment when you don't make the right choices.

Freedom is scary. You lose control over people when you set them free. They can do whatever they want and if they do something wrong and never have to pay for it, then what will keep them from doing wrong all the time?

∿—❦❦❦—∿

If you set up a system where there was a scale of crime versus penalty and you gave a fine according to the offense, the person would be focused on getting the penalty paid so that he could be free again. Punishments range from guilt and shame to time served and life lost. Over time, a person would learn behavior patterns that helped him avoid having to pay penalties. He's not a changed man. He is an educated man. He may want to do certain things that require a fine, but he refrains because he doesn't want to pay up.

Next you set up a new system where there was a list of crimes but no penalties. In this new system, the only crime that receives punishment is the crime of living like you were under the old system and if that's the case then the punishments are as listed. Under the new government, there is no risk of getting caught when committing a crime because even if a man is caught, there's no punishment.

With no penalty to center his focus and no need to focus on the list of crimes, the only direction for his mind to go is to his intentions. With no need to hide his crimes with more crimes, he can always live out in the open with nothing to fear or be ashamed of. He knows that he lives a guiltless existence by government decree, not by his own willpower. Knowing that he didn't earn his position keeps him from getting an inflated ego and feeling independent of the 'no blame' decree. If he decides to refrain from certain behaviors it's not because he has to or he's afraid not to. When he refrains from committing a crime, it's for no other reason but that he wants to.

The man is molded into who he was intended to be by a process of personal experience that was possible because of his freedom. He's a changed man and by disregarding the fear associated with breaking the rules he is freely conformed into what the rules intended him to be in the first place.

In both of these scenarios there is an opposing force or an evil foreign government that receives a pay off when a person pays their fines. Which scenario do you think the foreign organization would prefer you live or, at least, believe you live in?

The foreign government tries to get people to live like the old system yet believe that they are living the new system by tangling wording and muddling interpretation. The foreign regime takes advantage of the people's ignorance and steals from them.

What is worse is the people don't even think to escape and adopt the new government because they think they already have. They tell themselves that it's a wonderful existence because they know it's supposed to be.

It's similar to the children's story about the emperor and his new clothes. The tailors lied to the emperor and told him that only stupid and incompetent people would not be able to see the fabric of his new clothes. The king allowed himself to be dressed in the clothes and never admitted that he was too stupid and unfit to see them.

He paraded through the town in front of people who came out to see which of their neighbors were stupid and unfit. They remarked about the vibrant colors of the clothes and proclaimed their flamboyant beauty. They overcompensated because they were afraid to admit they couldn't see them.

It's the same psychology that makes a penniless man brag about his riches so that nobody can classify him as a poor person. What he doesn't realize is that the financially stable don't have to announce it because if they were to be investigated the truth would protect them.

Those with nothing to hide speak a lot less. Those who disregard the opinions of others speak the truth. A child who was watching the Kings procession through the streets spoke up and said, "But he's not wearing any clothes!"

This story is a metaphor for a situation where the overwhelming majority of witnesses willingly share in a combined ignorance of an obvious fact, despite individually recognizing the absurdity. The little boy's honesty, due to his disregard of judgment, deflates the pretentions of the king's court.

The tailors in this story and the foreign regime in my three-government analogy prey on pride and deep seeded desire to be honored and respected.

My three governments are a pretty simple representation of the old life before Jesus and the new life after Jesus. Before Jesus, we paid for our own sins. The list of crimes was put in place so that the people would know how to keep their lives in right relationship with God.

His ultimate desire is, simply, to have a relationship with His people. Behavior isn't His concern and owing a debt isn't what He's upset about. It's the gap between Himself and the people He loves that breaks His heart. So, He decided to pay the fines for everyone who ever existed in one shot.

In a lot of ways the religious people are like the emperor and the towns people. They pretentiously parade around loading people down with backpacks full of rules. "They seem to take pleasure in watching you stagger under these loads, and wouldn't think of lifting a finger to help. Their lives are perpetual fashion shows, embroidered prayer shawls one day and flowery prayers the next. They love to sit at the head table at church dinners, basking in the most prominent positions, preening in the radiance of public flattery, receiving honorary degrees, and getting called 'Doctor' and 'Reverend.'" (Jesus, Matthew 23:4-7)

The foreign regime is anyone, namely evil, that intends to keep people out of the life in Jesus and in the old government. They appear to be religious scholars. They mix the old with the new and their lives become walking contradictions. It's what Paul was talking about in Galatians 5:11-12 when he says, "If I were preaching that old message, no one would be offended if I mentioned the Cross now and then—it would be so watered-down it wouldn't matter one way or the other." You can whip up a trendy gourmet message of your own whims and feed it to the hungry masses without it occurring to a single unthinking listener that you have cancelled yourself out repeatedly and have ultimately said nothing.

My connection with Jesus is the only relationship that others have tried to take authority over. They set themselves up so that I would need to filter my thoughts and ideas through them and get their agreement before I could trust it. When I sinned, they used it as evidence against me that I never cared for Jesus in the first place. You cannot let people do that to you. "Don't set people up as experts over your life, letting them tell you what to do.

Save that authority for God; let him tell you what to do."
(Matthew 23:8)

I've always been turned off by the idea of religious
groups going out and recruiting people to their specific
style of religion. When they get a hold of the new recruit
they start imposing all of their beliefs and theories on
them without letting them live out their days in a natural
process of God discovery.

We're all unique. Why wouldn't you want a person to use their own unique approach to life and their
own experiences that develop into something authentic?
Why go to a third world country and teach them to hold a
praise and worship service that looks and sounds like the
one that you hold in the foothills of rural America? Why
can't they write their own praise songs with their own in-
struments from their own response to the revelations of
God?

I know that not all missions' trips are like this, but
there are too many to ignore that are. It's as though the
religious recruiters would rather groom the people for a
photo-op because that's what brings in the financial support and makes them look like saints. They 'go out into
all the world' to spread the air of religious American culture as though we're the standard. It's depersonalizing
and pompous. "You're hopeless, you religion scholars...
Frauds! You go halfway around the world to make a convert, but once you get him you make him into a replica of
yourselves, double-damned." (Jesus, Matthew 23:15)

In my own life, the people who seemed to be reli-
giously superior became roadblocks to me on my search
for the truth. The defining moments were when it was the
worst for all of us. The defining moments in anyone's life
are when you are at your worst. That's where you find out
where the lines are. If you demand penance of any kind
from a person who you've seen fail and withhold resto-

ration, reconciliation or any other representative action for forgiveness then you are a fraud. "Your lives are roadblocks to God's kingdom. You refuse to enter, and won't let anyone else in either." (Jesus, Matthew 23:13)

The differences between someone who lives under the old rule dominated government and a person who lives under a grace-dominated government are found when someone commits a crime. Whichever government they serve is the one they implement when the situation gets real. You can live in one or the other, but not both.

If you live your lives under one government, but claim the other then you cancel yourself out. You are either free or you're not. You are not free to be a slave. You are a slave to freedom. You don't avoid the crime to be free from punishment; you are free from the crime and consequently avoid the punishment.

I've always thought that if a person falls out of grace, then they have sinned. I have this mental picture of a bad apple falling out of a lush tree exposed and alone to rot on the ground while all of the other, bright shining apples enjoy life in the sun drenched tree. I thought that you were nestled in the lush leaves of grace and safely secured to the tree until you sinned and then you were out on your own.

Grace, by definition, is undeserved authentication of restoration and sanctification. That is a thesaurus-assisted way of saying that grace is an unfair gift of a new beginning and a clean slate. It's unfair because it goes to the undeserving. Simply put, grace is for sinners.

A person can follow the rules and busy themselves with the work of 'furthering the kingdom' and figuring out more 'relevant' ways to 'spread the good news,' but how can they "grow in grace"? (2 Peter 3:18) How do you grow in something that you are a part of only by failure? If grace exists only as a result of failure, then what good does it do to try to be good and follow a religious formula? When you cease to need grace because you've reached a place where you can maintain on your own then that is when you have fallen from grace.

"I suspect you would never intend this, but this is what happens. When you attempt to live by your own religious plans and projects, you are cut off from Christ, you fall out of grace. Meanwhile we expectantly wait for a satisfying relationship with the Spirit. For in Christ, neither our most conscientious religion nor disregard of religion amounts to anything. What matters is something far more interior: faith expressed in love." (Galatians 5:4-6)

There is no doubt that we have been given a life of freedom, but many try to re-tether themselves out of fear of failure. This fear comes from a misunderstanding of the basic principles of a life lived in Jesus. The thought process that leads to following a strict list of acceptable behaviors is the same thought process that would have you use your freedom as an excuse to do whatever you want. The root is the identical; they are both centered on self. Focus on self is the opposite of focus on God. When you live according to self, be it moral achievement or disregard for morality, you destroy your freedom.

If we're not using our freedom to get away with being selfish, then what is it for? We can't keep from sinning; we're not even supposed to develop a system to keep us from it. "...use your freedom to serve one another in love; that's how freedom grows. For everything we know about God's Word is summed up in a single sentence: Love others as you love yourself. That's an act of true freedom." (Galatians 5:13-14) For those who want to figure out a way to stand out as being one of the people who 'get it', "then step down. If you puff yourself up, you'll get the wind knocked out of you. But if you're content to simply be yourself, your life will count for plenty." (Jesus, Matthew 23:11-12)

chapter eighteen
greatest of these

"But the greatest of these is love." 1 Corinthians 13:13

Listen to the freethinking, intellectual minds throughout the centuries and hear them proclaim the need to question authority, think for themselves and pioneer new ideas. The half-embalmed anchors hold their place in the canal of tradition rather than continuing on course to the raging sea of water walkers. What they are not seeing is that questions are asked by those who know that they don't know everything. It's a position of humility and submission.

To search for meaning for yourself is to find a real and personal experience that becomes the make-up of who you are. The opposite would be the despicable regurgitation of what they've heard from everybody else, it's shallow and has no personal meaning and cannot save you when you find yourself in need of salvation.

I want to get you to think. I want to challenge you, to shake up your belief system. It's not my goal to turn you away from your faith in God, but rather to help you discover something authentic that will only increase your faith in God. I want you to reach a point that you cannot contain within yourself who God actually is. You can spend your whole life trying to, but it will keep spilling over and you'll only have the option of standing in awe of Him exclaiming your inexpressible praise to an uncontainable God. The I AM pours Himself into his fragile and imperfect creation and all of His creation cries out, "Holy, Holy, Holy, is the Lord Almighty!" (Isaiah 6:3)

I thought about naming this book 'Greatest of These' but, it's not something that I would have picked up off the shelf when I needed a book like this. I was scanning book covers for words that went straight to the point of my pain.

My goal is to find the people who are in a situation like I came from and need someone to reach down and help them to their feet. You can either learn from your mistakes or be crushed by them. I chose to learn. My responsibility, now, is to 'strengthen my brothers.'

There are many different directions for my thoughts to go when I think about strength, but as I've learned in this journey I'm on, things are not as they seem. I've seen so much damage that is done by well-meaning religion that I've developed an allergy to it. When I think of strength in terms of building you up and making you feel empowered, then I'd say that I have failed because all I've learned and all I've written are where we get it so devastatingly wrong.

However, if you understand strength in terms of scripture, then our personal strength is actually our disadvantage because God's "strength comes into its own in [our] weakness." (2 Corinthians 12:9) With this truth in mind, provided those who are solid in religion will let any of this penetrate their stubborn will, they will be strengthened by coming to terms with their weakness. Classically backward, confidence reversed.

Usually if you have someone telling you all of the places where you are deficient, it leads to a feeling of inadequacy. However, if you think about the way the Bible tells us to view our abilities, it is precisely that. Flip everything you are confident about knowing and be certain that you know very little.

A person who is confident that they don't have the whole story will pay sharp attention to their surroundings. They won't jump to conclusions and start making angry allegations. This puts you in line with scripture. "Everyone should be quick to listen, slow to speak and slow to become angry." (James 1:19 NIV) Proverbs 14:29 says that people who do the opposite store up 'stockpiles of stupidity' and Proverbs 19:11 says, "Smart people know how to hold their tongue; their grandeur is to forgive and forget." Grandeur is another word for dignity. How backward it is to be more dignified in forgiving than in winning.

Out of every instruction that has been written in the scriptures, the most important thing we can do is love one another. If we have done no other act in our lives except give love, then we have accomplished more than anyone else ever could. "If I give everything I own to the poor and even go to the stake to be burned as a martyr, but I don't love, I've gotten nowhere. So, no matter what I say, what I believe, and what I do, I'm bankrupt without love." (1 Corinthians 13:3)

Jesus, in John 15:17, calls loving one another the 'root command.' Maybe this is the case because if we treat others like we would want to be treated, then our lives would line up with the law code without even trying. "When you love others you complete what the law has been after all along." (Romans 13:8) This makes sense because when you go through the Ten Commandments you can see how those things could be avoided simply by loving others the way you would love yourself. "You can't go wrong when you love others. When you add up everything in the law code, the sum total is love." (Romans 13:10)

Love isn't a natural reaction in most cases because it goes against our human nature. Simply telling someone that they have to love others leaves too much up to their own interpretation. There is a checklist in 1 Corinthians 13 that you can reference if you're not sure how to respond with love in a particular situation. There are sixteen characteristics of love listed and a few of my favorites are: love never gives up, doesn't keep score of the sins of others, puts up with anything, trusts God always, always looks for the best, never looks back but keeps going to the end.

Something about love is that it leaves you painfully vulnerable. Love can cause you to put yourself in a position of submission and humility. When you give love with no promise of return, you are consenting to being hurt. Few people who I know would put self-preservation aside and open themselves up in that way. It would be viewed as foolish and risky. If we are vessels who are fashioned to be used by God in any way that He has purpose for, then our interjections only get in the way of the free flowing liquid movement that God pours through us. Our right to our selves has been relinquished, or so we say, but when it comes down to the wire, the truth will be told by how we respond in the moment.

The thing that sets believers apart from a non-believing world is found in 1 John 3:14, "The way we know we've been transferred from death to life is that we love our brothers and sisters. Anyone who doesn't love is as good as dead." It's the ultimate guideline. If you measure your life by love, then you'll get it right every time. "The whole point of what we're urging is simply love — love uncontaminated by self-interest and counterfeit faith, a life open to God. Those who fail to keep to this point soon wander off into cul-de-sacs of gossip. They set themselves up as experts on religious issues, but haven't the remotest idea of what they're holding forth with such imposing eloquence." (1 Timothy 1:5)

Of all the possible reasons that love is such an emphasis in the Bible I believe the main reason is found in 1 John 4:8 and 16, "God is love." You can't know God if you don't love. Romans chapter thirteen says that you can't go wrong with love and it's confirmed in 1 John chapter 4 where it says that if you let love have the run of the house then you have no fear of judgment.

Love sucks the power out of sin and conquers evil. When you choose to let love flow through you and be the only thing that initiates any kind of action from you, then you will always come out on top. Sin has the potential to breed more sin. This process has been paralleled to the effect of yeast in a bread recipe. A small amount of yeast quickly spreads through the entire loaf of bread. One person can sin and the domino effect of responses breeds more sin, permeating the entire group. "Most of all, love each other as if your life depended on it. Love makes up for practically anything." (1 Peter 4:8)

In my story, my own choices initiated fallout of more sin. Hurt, when mixed with stubborn pride and a lack of understanding of God's absolute authority, becomes a numbing agent in the barometer of the spirit. You are supposed to deny the urges of your flesh, be it self-gratification or self-preservation, but one of the hardest things to ignore is the sting in your flesh from the slap that sin delivered.

Sin does not touch the spirit. Sin deals only with death. When you respond to sin with more sin, you are gratifying the self and it's the worst when it's under the guise of religious preservation. You say you are standing up for what is right, but what you're doing is cancelling out the possibility for restoration and completeness under supernatural grace. Sin hurts the physical body, yet you strike out against the spirit out of the misunderstanding that someone who actually loved God would never find themselves entangled in sin.

When a man stands in front of you, you see the man. He has flaws, personality quirks, annoying idiosyncrasies, moral weakness and holes in his integrity even if they're only found buried in his intentions. When he becomes a believer he is still the man with the flaws, only now he has the spirit of God inside of him. When he fails, it's his flawed body that is failing, not the spirit within him. If his identity is now the new man made one with Jesus and that identity is trapped in the body of the old man, then who do you punish when he sins? Do you speak your harsh words to him, the inner man who is tangled with Jesus, or do you address the old man, the body?

A person is either alive in Christ or dead in sin. If they are not a believer, then your words do not apply to them. They live under a different jurisdiction and you are speaking a language that they cannot understand. You cannot place judgment on them and you have no authority over them whatsoever. If they are a believer, then when you speak to them, you are speaking to Jesus. Paul says in Galatians 2:20 that it is not him that lives, but Christ that lives in him. If this is the case, then the words you speak and the things you do are done to Jesus. "When you hurt your friend, you hurt Christ." (1 Corinthians 8:12)

I have to deal with my own sin when I read that. I have to deal with the fact that I defiled Jesus in more ways than one. I defiled Him in my own body, I defiled Him in another's body and I hurt Him when I hurt all of the fringe people who were affected. What a load of debt.

What an excessive gift of grace to erase that sin.

It's your turn now. Now that you know that whatever you do to the least of us, you do to Jesus, what are you going to do? What changes are you going to make? Is there some rephrasing that you would like to do or a message that you would like to retract? In this bizarre world of Christianity that we live in, we have given up our rights to ourselves. Our bodies do not get a say in our conscious choices, we no longer belong to ourselves.

If someone found themselves in need of my forgiveness, I would have no choice but to forgive them. If I didn't, there would be a battle inside of my body that I would have to find ways to live with and that would chip away at my freedom.

What's more powerful in me is the life-size memory of my own overwhelming need for forgiveness and an irresistible urge compels me to be lavish with my own measure of love. "Great gifts mean greater responsibilities."(Luke 12:48)

Getting mad at a man of flesh and blood for sinning is the same as getting mad at a one year old for soiling her diaper. She's wearing a diaper because she cannot physically control the muscles responsible for making her diaper dirty. We are covered by grace because we cannot physically control the nature responsible for making us dirty. Much like a diaper makes the clean up a lot quicker, love makes our restoration complete.

Picture this giant tower made out of people grasping hands and supporting feet on their shoulders and their feet being supported by someone else's shoulders. We make this massive tower of bodies that are emptied of a say-so and are simply vessels for God to pour Himself into to conduct His business through. The bodies still twitch with decisions and urges and make attempts to disrupt the flow of Love between the vessels.

One body hurts another and asks for forgiveness, the body next to it says they forgive, but is not interested in restoring relationship and sets their body up to maintain its own without acknowledging the one next to it. There is a weak spot in the fabric and the flow of Love has been cut off between those two people. This tower makes up the body of Christ and, when you stand there refusing to heal the wound that sin caused, can you not smell the rank breath of the roaring lion as he roams to and fro sniffing out the stubbornly upright to use their indignation to destroy them?

When a follower of Christ, an identity that is one with Jesus, sins, it is not the person who is sinning. It is the body that they live in that is sinning. Paul says in Romans chapter seven that when he does something that he knows is wrong it is no longer he that does it, but the sin that lives in him that does it. In spite of knowing right from wrong and wanting desperately to always do right, we are not a hundred percent in control of ourselves. The sin in our bodies rebelliously trips up our best intentions and takes charge.

When this happened to me, I found myself wanting out of this body. Sexual sins are the worst because it's the body that commits them and you can't escape your body except through death. This isn't to be confused with suicidal thoughts that stem from self-pity, this is a knowing that my body is a chamber of sin and I, the inner self that is joined with Jesus, wanted out. If my relationship, devotion and love for Jesus weren't enough to keep me from the burning passions of sin, then what am I to do?

I spent countless nights begging God to let me wake up one morning and I would be backward in time and it would be months earlier and I could make different choices and avoid the destruction that I caused. For a long time I felt like I was in the middle of a bad dream and it would only be a matter of time and I could wake up and it would all be over. I wanted to go home, but my home was gone.

I was a refugee of sin sleeping in the streets of uncertainty mourning my own death and shivering with fear that I would have to live out the rest of my days tossed out of the presence of God. He held me close as the darkness of night sent its bitter wind to lick my naked skin. He rocked me in His arms and whispered, 'Don't let your faith fail, my little girl, my love is bigger than this. Be still, little one, and know that I am God. You don't have to be afraid, lamb, you may have lost many, but you won't lose me. I could never forget you. I've engraved your name on the palms of my hands. I can take care of this. I'll make this right.' (Luke 22:31, 2 Corinthians 12:9, Psalm 46:10, Isaiah 54:10, Isaiah 49:16, Romans 8:28)

As it stands today, the people who I have hurt have made a series of decisions that result in a separation between them and us. I must admit that Justin got the worse end of the deal. I have simply ceased to exist in the eyes of many. Justin, on the other hand, has been dehumanized. The very blood that makes him a father has been drained from his veins and his voice has been removed from the ears that are connected to the hard hearts that isolate his daughter in a world without grace.

The world is not surprised when they hear of the divided families, the severed lives and denial of reconciliation. The world is not surprised because that is exactly what they would have done. There is no message there, nothing to learn in the norm. What if they were to get up from the floor, wipe the blood dripping from their nose and offer us a seat at their table? What uproar the world would make. 'Are you crazy?' they would ask. "What on earth compels you to open your doors to the people who hurt you so much?"

What a story of impact that would be. What a way to demonstrate what you believe Jesus did for every single one of us. How would you explain the grace and mercy that you show? Now that's a story. Think of the lives you would be saving and changing by simply putting the faith that you proclaim with your mouth into action when the situation is real. Your crazy act of grace would get the town talking. Instead of perpetuating the sin of another, making yourself look good and justified, you would be perpetuating the love of Jesus, making yourself appear unworldly and your faith absolutely compelling.

I have spent the last two years pouring over scriptures, books and anything else I could get my hands on to make a case for grace. The overall message, I believe, is that we don't have enough information to do anything but love one another and do everything within our power to stay together. There is an evil that has saturated the churchy culture and dressed itself up in whatever you would be inclined to respond to. Keep your faith simple, do what you can to not hurt each other or yourself. When you fall, get up. If you see someone fall, don't run from him out of fear, stand by him and help him fight off the attack. Remember, it's not about the man, there's a bigger picture. Things aren't as they seem.

There is so much that we don't know. "We only know a portion of the truth, and what we say about God is always incomplete." (1 Corinthians 13:9) There is so much we don't see. "We don't see things clearly. We are squinting in a fog, peering through a mist." (1 Corinthians 13:12) So, 'for right now we have three things to lead us: trust steadily in God, hope unswervingly and love extravagantly. The greatest of these is love.' (1 Corinthians 13:13) Love wins *every* time.

afterword

One of the biggest challenges for me while writing this book was to know that I am capturing a period of time and setting it in a stone that can be seen long after I'm gone. Long after the circumstance has been reconciled.

Humanity is perfectly imperfect and when you take a snapshot of life before it has a chance to get dressed for the occasion, you're going to see the flaws. I've taken a snapshot of a group of people when they were not dressed for the part. It's gritty. It's unfair. But, it's real.

The characters in my story, though slightly shrouded by their own obscurity in the big picture and the name change, are real people with real flaws, but with real potential.

Twenty years from now, when everyone has been reconciled, I want to be proud of what I've written in these pages.

I don't know if I've done that, but it's been a priority.

Marc is now married to a woman who calls him her 'Prince Charming.'

Madeline escaped the small town and its watchful eye and lives in the big city doing the corporate thing. She and I are friends and, though we may never stay up all night drinking coffee and singing Madonna songs again, we'll never fully be rid of the sisterhood that we share.

Diane has always been a woman who wants to make a difference. I believe that she will.

Mitch has not been portrayed in the best light in

my life, but deep down, I believe that he truly wants to be a powerful force in the eyes of God. Some of the biggest mistakes are made by the bravest in heart. His story is not over.

Anne is a woman of strength. She is someone to be looked up to. I hate being the one who hurt her so deeply.

Justin continues to receive promises that he can see his daughter...eventually.

credits

Chapter 5: Hell '05

>Mitch's letter was an e-mail sent with the subject,
>*"A long note from an old friend..."* Content has been
>reduced to protect identities and unnecessary hurt
>to unrelated people.

Chapter 6: Ode to Mrs. Moore

>"When Godly People Do Ungodly Things"
>Written by Beth Moore
>Broadman & Holman Publishers
>ISBN 0805424652
>Pages: 4, 13, 14, 89, 90, 92 and 93
>Duplicated and used by permission.

Chapter 10: Dusty Religion

>"The Kingdom of God is Within You"
>Written by Leo Tolstoy
>Barnes and Noble Books, Ny
>ISBN 0760765529
>Pages: 50, 51
>Used by permission.

Chapter 15: Role Playing

>"Rumors Of Another World: What On Earth Are
>We Missing?"
>Written by Philip Yancey
>Zondervan

ISBN 0310252172
Pages: 28, 29
Used by permission from Mr. Yancey.

"The Lion, the Witch and the Wardrobe"
Written by C.S. Lewis
Copyright C.S. Lewis Pte. Ltd. 1950
ISBN 006070764899
Page: 81
Extract reprinted by permission.

Consider going through 'Grace Is For Sinners' with your Bible study, small group or book club.

Write a book review for your favorite publication, local newspaper or web site. Ask your local radio station to interview the author. Media often pay more attention to their readers and listeners than they do publicists and authors.

If you are a store owner and would like to carry copies of this book to sell in your store, email info@graceisforsinners.com to find out about our discounted rates for resale items.

Talk about the book with your friends, church group and online community. Engage people in conversation and recommend this book for those you think might be encouraged or challenged.

If you know someone whose voice is heard by a wider group of people, ask them to review a copy of this book and talk about it to their audience.

www.graceisforsinners.com

read it again.

CPSIA information can be obtained at www.ICGtesting.com
Printed in the USA
LVOW13s1210030614

388406LV00001B/75/P